HOLLYWOOD

AND THE AMERICAN IMAGE

HOLLYWOOD
AND THE AMERICAN IMAGE

BY TONY THOMAS

ARLINGTON HOUSE Westport, Connecticut

First published in 1981 by Arlington House/Publishers, 333 Post
Road West, Westport, Connecticut 06880.

This book was produced for Arlington House/Publishers by
Rosebud Books
A Division of The Knapp Press
5455 Wilshire Boulevard
Los Angeles, California 90036

Design by Michael Burke

Library of Congress Cataloging in Publication Data

Thomas, Tony, 1927 –
Hollywood and the American image.

Bibliography: p.
Includes index.
1. National characteristics, American, in motion pictures. I. Title.
PN1995.9.N34T5   791.43'09'093520313   81-3626
ISBN 0-87000-525-1   AACR2

Printed in the United States of America

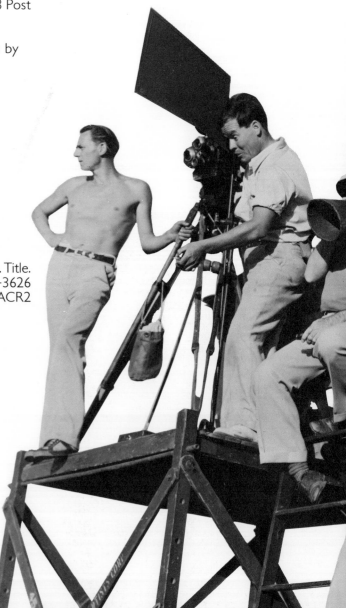

For Andrea

ACKNOWLEDGMENT

In preparing much of the research for this book, I am, as on many previous occasions, indebted to the library of the Academy of Motion Picture Arts and Sciences (Beverly Hills), and the help graciously given by Mrs. Terry Roach and her staff. In collecting the illustrations my thanks go to Eddie Brandt and Mike Hawks of *Saturday Matinee* (North Hollywood); Paula Klaw of *Movie Star News* (New York); Bob Colman of the *Hollywood Poster Exchange* (Los Angeles); Ron Haver, director of film programming at the Los Angeles County Museum of Art; Mike Snell, Lesley Anderson Snell, and the Museum of Modern Art film stills archives (New York). Finally, a word of thanks to my editor, Bo Hathaway, for his help and guidance.

King Vidor directing an outdoor scene from Our Daily Bread.

Errol Flynn as George Armstrong Custer in Warner Bros.' version of the famous last stand: They Died with Their Boots On, 1941.

CONTENTS

Carole Lombard and Fred MacMurray, the devoted couple in Swing High, Swing Low.

Youthful, kinetic American energy: Judy Garland and Mickey Rooney in Strike Up the Band.

INTRODUCTION

A MIRROR FOR AMERICA

I may never have become an American had it not been for Hollywood. My curiosity about America was born in English movie theatres, particularly in the three or four theatres in the town of Deal, near Dover, in Kent, where at the age of ten I discovered westerns. For several years that was the only kind of film that really interested me, which did not make me very different from my chums except that they seemed to regard what they saw on the screen as merely abstract entertainment, whereas I liked to ponder about these pictures. I even listed them in a notebook – under the names of the stars: Buck Jones, Ken Maynard, Tim McCoy, John Wayne, et al. They were so different from my own people, and so was the scenery in which they functioned. Those wide, open spaces, those rocky mountains and endless plains looked like views of another planet to a boy used to the neat, green, damp fields of Kent. And for a boy who hated the cold the fact that westerns took place in weather that was invariably warm and sunny made them even more fascinating. I knew that I *had* to see that country.

It was my good fortune to have my dreams come true. Many years later, as a journalist and broadcaster, I would come to know some of the men I had idolized as a youngster. I would never

9

John Wayne with Sheila Manners in Westward Ho, *1935; Tim McCoy in* Fighting for Justice, *1933; Buck Jones with John Elliot in* Smoke Tree Range, *1937; Ken Maynard with Ruth Hall in* Strawberry Roan, *1933.*

meet Buck Jones, who topped my list. He died a hero's death in Boston in 1942, rescuing people from a fire. But I would later be responsible for hiring Ken Maynard and Tim McCoy for television appearances. Maynard would prove to be a sad experience for me. He had lived improvidently and he had nothing left, except a great desire to drink. It was uncomfortable to be around him. Colonel McCoy on the other hand was a living marvel. He was warm and witty and highly knowledgeable about western history. Some of the most enjoyable evenings of my life have been those I spent with him at his home in Nogales, Arizona, listening to his own involvement with the Indians and the army in the West.

As one of the writers of the 1979 Academy Awards show it was my job to write John Wayne's material. Sadly, it proved to be his last public appearance. As I sat in the theatre, the Dorothy Chandler Pavilion at the Music Center in Los Angeles, listening to him read my lines, my thoughts went back to 1937 and some of the titles I had listed under his name: *Winds of the Wasteland, Lawless Range,* and *The Lonely Trail.* It was difficult not to feel a little bit self-satisfied. Mine had been a celluloid odyssey.

My boyish yen for westerns gradually blossomed into an interest in other kinds of movies. In the late summer of 1939, age twelve, two things happened to change my life a little. War broke out in Europe – and I fell in love with Deanna Durbin when I saw her in the aptly titled *First Love.* I saw all of her pictures after that. And my curiosity about America grew. The settings of her movies were so nice. Nice houses and streets and nice people. Years later I would come to know some of those streets and houses on the back lot at Universal, just as I would discover that the New York byways of the James Cagney gangster epics were actually in Burbank. My entire concept of the American West, it turned out, came from the use of the west end of the San Fernando Valley and the Santa Susanna Pass leading into the Simi Valley – within thirty miles of Hollywood. Almost all the B westerns were shot on those locations. Today both valleys are full of housing tracts and whenever I drive over the pass I look up into the hills, hoping for a glimpse of the ghosts of Jones, McCoy, and Maynard galloping on their white horses. I peer into the smoggy haze in vain.

As I progressed through my teenage years my interest in America expanded with an average of two weekly visits to the movies, and in those days they were always double bills, complete with newsreels and shorts. It was all fodder for a mind eager to learn more about that fascinating land on the other side of the Atlantic. I recall being astounded by the vitality of Mickey

11

Claude Rains as
the doomed Dr. Towers
in Kings Row.

12

Fredric March as the avuncular Mark Twain.

Rooney and Judy Garland in *Strike Up the Band*. Were all American kids, I wondered, that full of pep and enterprise? Later on I would wonder if life in St. Louis, Missouri, was as warmly convivial as Vincente Minnelli made it out to be in *Meet Me in St. Louis*, or whether middle-class life in the States was as splendidly tightly knit as in *Since You Went Away*. I was eager to believe that it was all true.

Hollywood dealt with the darker aspects of American life, particularly crime, but the antics of crooks and hoods never appealed to me. I was much more intrigued with the dark side of romantic Americana, such as *King's Row, The House of the Seven Gables*, and *Dragonwyck*. I was greatly impressed with John Ford's rather macabre western *My Darling Clementine* and resolved to one day visit the place in which its story was set – Tombstone, Arizona. When I finally turned up in Tombstone I realized that Ford had shot the picture up in Monument Valley, on the northern boundary of Arizona and not in Tombstone, which is near Mexico. But it didn't matter. I saw both Tombstone and Monument Valley, and much of the rest of that fantastic state.

By the time I saw James Cagney as George M. Cohan in *Yankee Doodle Dandy* and Fredric March acting out *The Adventures of Mark Twain*, I was ready to write to the American Embassy in London and ask about emigrating. In fact, I did, but it was still wartime, and I was advised it would be a long time before a young man such as myself would likely be able to make the crossing. So I kept going to the movies, absorbing impressions, dreaming, and pondering.

The true value of all this time spent in the dark was not so much what I learned from what I saw but what I learned from the subsequent trips to the library in search of further facts. My curiosity was whetted by the people, places, and things touched upon by the movies, even if they were treated superficially. For example, my idolization of Errol Flynn caused me to see *They Died With Their Boots On* many times and become curious about George Armstrong Custer. On my first trip out West in the summer of 1948 nothing could stop me visiting the site of that famous Last Stand. The same picture also triggered an interest in the Civil War and a desire to travel through the South. Soon I became immersed in a study of American history, culture, and geography. I was stimulated by these Hollywood concoctions of America, and I liked what I saw. It led me to believe that my destiny lay on the western side of the Atlantic.

I do not regret my decision. Indeed, I still feel grateful to the old Hollywood. I stress the *old* because there is not much I like about the Hollywood of today, although I am grateful that it is the community in which I make my living. For the most part I do not

Yankee Doodle Dandy personified: James Cagney as George M. Cohan in Warner Bros.' colorful account of the composer and song-and-dance man. Cagney's real sister Jean (left) played Cohan's sister. Joan Leslie played his wife Mary, and Walter Houston and Rosemary De Camp were the senior Cohans. Released in 1942, the film well matched the patriotic spirit of the time.

John Wayne as Quirt Evans, the badman redeemed by the angel, in Angel and the Badman.

like the image it projects of America and its people. If I were a teenager in another country today, I wonder if I would be sparked to want to be an American by what I saw on the screens, both the large ones and the small ones? It is impossible to give a true answer. My values and views are those of another time.

As this book goes to press in 1981, more than half of the features made in Hollywood require restricted ratings. The films are restricted because they deal with sex and violence in a brutally graphic manner and because the language of the gutter is now the *lingua franca* of the screen. Sex and violence have been basic ingredients of the movies ever since cameras started to turn, but in previous times the strictures of censorship limited the range of depiction. But the censorship was so unreasonable, so puritanical it had to go. Most people agreed with that stand, but a few shook their heads. Do away with the rules and the sluice gates of filth will open up! Impossible, the majority countered. The basic good taste and moral concern within the industry will prevail and the producers will be their own censors. Alas, the majority proved to be naive. Quo Vadis, America?

The America of Hollywood's Golden Age – an arbitrary time period but usually considered to be from the early thirties to the late forties – was hardly ever projected on the screen with reality. Film is fantasy. Not even newsreels and documentaries are reality because their content and impact are limited by what is captured by the camera and by how the images are edited. Films are made because it is in someone's interest to make them. If they entertain or enlighten they do so peripherally. Their primary purpose is to make money. Hollywood was never benign or beneficent. It never will be. The danger is, at least in the eyes of this lifetime observer and reporter, that Hollywood has become dominated by men who are more interested in making money than in making good films. Hopefully there are, and always will be, people who believe in art as well as commerce and who also believe that as creators of entertainment they have a responsibility to the public, to themselves, to their country, to the general good.

I was to learn, once I crossed the Atlantic, that all Americans are not as philosophical as Will Rogers, as funny as Bob Hope, as brave as John Wayne, as gentlemanly as Randolph Scott, as suave as William Powell, as upright as Gary Cooper, as genial as James Stewart, as scintillating as Carole Lombard or as lovely as Irene Dunne. But in my travels – and my curiosity led me to every part of the country – I found Americans with bits and pieces of all those qualities, and more. The land was more vast and varied than Hollywood had led me to believe, the history was more complex and interesting, and the potential for a good life even greater. My own American Dream was not a disappointment, and I cannot forget that it was a dream that started in England because of seeing movies made in Hollywood. The films and actors discussed in this book are a cross section of what I saw before leaving my native land and of what intrigued me about America and Americans. I can but hope the reader will share some of that enjoyment, that fascination with past but lingering American images.

Tony Thomas

ONE

ROOTS
OF
GRASS

Will Rogers (left) and with Charley Grapewin (above) in Judge Priest.

The American Image propagated by the movies in Hollywood's Golden Age was always more rural than urban. The movie moguls took their cue from Abraham Lincoln and celebrated the qualities of the common people rather than the leaders of society and the captains of industry. They also saw the value in playing up the virtues outlined in the Bill of Rights, especially those pertaining to individualism and the right of the individual to make his own way in life, and those virtues tended to look better when set in America's hamlets and byways and wide open spaces rather than its cities. Hence the universal popularity of the western. Horace Greeley (1811-1872) greatly influenced Hollywood thinking with his advice to young men about going West. What an injustice that the movie moguls never saw fit to make a movie about this crusading journalist, political activist, abolitionist, free-land advocate, and labor organizer. James Cagney would have made a marvelous Greeley. Justice, of course, was never a factor in Hollywood thinking and is never likely to be. Hollywood is Business. Fortunately, in that Golden Age, it was good business to play up what was good about America rather than what was bad, and the good Amer-

Rogers as widower Judge Priest giving his
ritual morning greeting to his deceased
wife's photo.

(Right)
Rogers with Anita Louise and with Tom
Brown.

ican image of personal freedom and fair treatment looked
particularly good set in a small town and personified by a genial
fellow like Will Rogers.

The American image was never more beautifully treated
than in the three films John Ford made with Rogers: *Dr.
Bull* (1933), *Judge Priest* (1934), and *Steamboat Round the Bend*
(1935). It was an ideal blending of two talents. In the first picture
Rogers was a town doctor in a small Connecticut community
sometime in the early twenties, in the second he is a judge in
a small Kentucky town, circa 1890, and in the third he is a would-
be Mississippi riverboat captain of about the same era. In all he
is as he always was – a walking slice of genial, homespun Americana, with a savvy awareness of human nature and a limitless
fund of common sense. It is difficult to assess Rogers as an actor;
all that need be said is that he played Will Rogers wonderfully
well. John Ford had no need to be told this. In all his films with

Rogers he directed him to be himself, to use the script only as a guideline and to invent his own dialogue. Of the three films the one which gets closer to Rogers as a man is *Judge Priest*. Here he is the basically decent man, a moralist but without pretension, a fixer-upper, a balancer, and the exorciser of whatever evil influences creep into his bailiwick. With Rogers it was hard to tell where the man left off and the image started.

Will Rogers was born in the Oklahoma Territory in 1879, and among his bloodlines was a strong strain of Cherokee. During his early years he was a cowboy and learned the riding and the roping that became such essential parts of his act as an entertainer. At the age of twenty he got a job on a boat that delivered mules to the British Army in South Africa, and it was in Johannesburg that he first appeared in a Wild West show – as the rope-twirling Cherokee Kid. Back in America he joined another traveling show, and in 1904 he could be seen spinning his ropes at

After his acquittal Bob Gillis (David Landau) carries the flag, joining Judge Priest and the townspeople in a parade of southern pride.

the St. Louis World's Fair. From there he graduated to the vaudeville circuit, chewing gum and spinning his lariat but never saying anything. One day, when a trick went wrong, Rogers did say something and the audience laughed. So he kept dropping ad-lib comments into his act, and with time it developed into a monologue, complete with rope tricks. The public loved to hear his earthy but incisive opinions of current affairs, particularly politics. The cracker-barrel wit appealed to even the sophisticates, and Rogers found himself one of the stars of *The Ziegfeld Follies of 1917*. A year later he was in Hollywood at the invitation of Samuel Goldwyn and became the star of *Laughing Bill Hyde*.

Silent movies of the early twenties did not give Rogers the setting his humor needed. His pithy comments appeared as subtitles, but without his drawling delivery they lacked bite. So he drifted back to New York and more appearances with the Follies. He also started to get into print with humorous articles and went out on his first lecture tour. Rogers the Cowboy Pundit had slowly taken form and now he was a very distinct entity. The *Saturday Evening Post* sent him to Europe in 1927 to do a string of commentaries, and when he returned home he went back to Hollywood as the star of *A Texas Steer*, which presented him as a cowboy who becomes a Congressman and brings a little horse sense to Washington. But the outlet Rogers needed was sound, and once that came into being his career in Hollywood really took flight. His first sound film was *They Had to See Paris* in 1929, for which he was paid $50,000. It did so well Fox put him under contract and gave him $60,000 for the next one. And so it went. On the radio and in the newspaper he was nothing less than a political commentator, and his influence had much to do with the election of Franklin Delano Roosevelt to the White House in 1932. He was also by this time in the top ten at the movie box office. Films like *State Fair*, *David Harum*, and *Handy Andy* brought huge returns for Fox, and when John Ford asked for Rogers for *Dr. Bull* the studio was delighted to bring the two talents together. They were even happier when Ford and Rogers decided to do *Judge Priest*, using the stories of Irvin S. Cobb, who himself was very happy to have his material used by two such figures.

Judge Priest is more the study of the character of a small Kentucky town than it is a story – and the main character in that town is its wise, paternal judge, Billy Priest, a widower who now and then chats with the portrait of his beloved wife and reports on the comings and goings of the population. His nephew Jerome (Tom Brown) is a newly appointed lawyer who is in love with the beautiful Ellie May Gillespie (Anita Louise) but is unhappy because the townspeople look with disdain upon her. Ellie seems to have no family background and they feel a lawyer should do

Bob Gillis (center) is saved by the testimony of a southern gentleman (Henry B. Walthall, right).

On the set with director John Ford; Rogers; Dorothy Arzner, then Hollywood's only woman director; and author Irvin S. Cobb.

better for himself. She doesn't even know who her father was. But she is about to find out. Bob Gillis (David Landau) is a mysterious drifter who hits a man when he makes a sneering remark about Ellie. The man's friends gang up on Gillis, who cuts one of them with a knife in defending himself and is arrested. He refuses to say why he took offense at hearing Ellie, actually his daughter, slighted. Jerome takes the case for the defense, but since it is election time and political feelings are acute, the forces who oppose Judge Priest demand that he surrender his chair to another judge for this case because Jerome is his nephew. Hurt at this aspersion on his integrity, Judge Priest nevertheless appoints a substitute.

The Reverend Ashby Brand (Henry B. Walthall) calls Judge Priest for a conference one evening and reveals some unknown facts to him. The reverend was an officer in the Confederate Army, and he is willing to appear in court in defense of Gillis. By a ruse he and the judge get the case reopened. The reverend tells how Gillis was a member of a chain gang during the Civil War but volunteered to fight for the South, which he did with great bravery. The jury need hear no more – Gillis is acquitted. Judge Priest is reelected and makes it possible for Jerome and Ellie to marry, now that she has been united with her vindicated father, no longer a drifter with a dark past but a new citizen of the town.

The two main assets of Judge Priest are its star and its director. John Ford liked the material so much that he remade it twenty years later as The Sun Shines Bright, casting the lovable Charles Winninger as Billy Priest. But the first version retains its own values despite the better visual and harder hitting elements of the second, which was able to deal more frankly with racial issues and prejudice among the townspeople. Judge Priest is a warm piece of Fordian Americana, conveying the fierce pride and Confederate consciousness that persisted thirty years after the war. As the judge, Will Rogers played a combination of himself, with his own brand of folksy wit and wisdom, and the warmly wise character created by Irvin S. Cobb. It was a powerful combination and it was among the finest pieces of work Rogers ever did on the screen.

Judge Priest proved that Will Rogers was not merely a charming and comedic figure but a man who had mastered the camera and knew how to sustain a convincing character. It is sad to think what more he might have achieved as an actor had he lived. He made five more films, the last of them being Ford's Steamboat Round the Bend, but before it was released he was killed in an airplane crash in Alaska. He was fifty-six. America was stunned by the loss. He had become a cracker-barrel philosopher, a sort of Oklahoma Socrates, whose comments on the American way of life were welcomed in the newspapers and on the airwaves as a national, humorous balance wheel. And Hollywood lost one of its most popular stars.

24

Hollywood in its Golden Age seldom, if ever, regarded itself as a social instrument. Its reaction to the Great Depression was to virtually ignore it and turn out entertainment that would take the country's mind off its economic problems. The wealthy were frequently lampooned in lightheaded comedies; the studios accented glamour and romance, and encouraged daydreaming with such flights of fancy as the Busby Berkeley musicals. Any producer or director who wanted to deal with the hunger and misery caused by the Depression had a hard time getting financing, as King Vidor found when he wanted to make *Our Daily Bread*. The track record of this superb director was firm even in 1934; born in Texas in 1894, he was making movies by the age of twenty, and by the time he directed *The Big Parade* in 1925 he was marked as one of America's most important directors. Such films as *The Crowd* (1928), *Hallelujah!* (1929), *The Champ* (1932), and *Bird of Paradise* (1932) steadily built his reputation. And yet, for all that, Vidor could not raise the backing to make *Our Daily Bread*.

Vidor was struck with the idea of a film which would inspire Americans by reinforcing their own image as do-it-yourselfers and remind them of their forefathers who had wrestled the wilderness and built a nation. The idea of the film came to him when he read a *Reader's Digest* article about cooperative farming.

The rest of the inspiration for the script and characters simply came from reading the daily newspapers. Vidor took his completed script to various studios, starting with MGM, for whom he made several profitable pictures, but they all turned him down. His friend Charlie Chaplin, who not only liked the script but contributed a number of ideas, arranged a United Artists releasing contract, and with that Vidor went to the banks. But one of the vital dramatic points in *Our Daily Bread* is the factor of foreclosure, to which the bankers objected, and because he would not alter the script Vidor could get no bank financing. Finally he decided to raise the money by mortgaging his home and personal property and in that way came up with $125,000, which was about half the usual budget for feature films, but with a sympathetic cast and crew he was able to make the film.

The two main characters, John and Mary Sims (Tom Keene and Karen Morley), were taken from Vidor's *The Crowd*. They are a young married couple badly hit by the Depression and who leave the city and move to a broken-down, bankrupt farm which they have inherited. John is totally ignorant of how to work the land, but a drifting Swedish farmer, Chris (John Qualen), drops by, and John invites him and his family to move in and help run the place. It then occurs to them to expand the idea and invite other kinds of workers and craftsmen to settle on the property and

Karen Morley and Tom Keene, the lovers in Our Daily Bread, *cross to their squatters' shack.*

The idealistic Keene addressing a co-op meeting.

King Vidor (in pullover) directing Our Daily Bread.

develop it into a co-op. Eventually about a hundred people, all of them desperate in their need to find work and a way of maintaining their families, pool their abilities and turn it into a functioning community, with John as their leader.

It is subsistence but at least it is life and work, as they till the land and live in their shelters. The skeleton society rallies when faced with a crisis – the land is foreclosed and a sheriff attempts to sell the farm at a public auction, but the squatters manage to exclude outside bidding and obtain title to the land with the small amount of money they raise between them. The real enemy is the climate and the nature of the land itself. Drought brings grief as their crops fail and wither for lack of water. On the personal level there is crisis with the leader. John has come under the spell of a pretty young blonde (Barbara Pepper) and prepares to leave with her. The plight of his fellow citizens brings him to his senses, and he stays. Discovering that there is a stream running through the hills a few miles from the farm, he rallies his men with his idea of digging an irrigation ditch from the stream, through the rugged terrain of the hills, and down into their fields. By great effort the scheme is brought to fruition, and the crops are saved, as is the community.

The digging of the irrigation ditch is the highlight of *Our Daily Bread* and one of the most stimulating and effective sequences ever achieved on the American screen. The factor of time is elemental in the sequence because the crops are close to dying. Dozens and dozens of men hack out the ditch with picks, shovels, sledgehammers, stakes, and even their bare hands. At points where the water must pass over ditches and gullies they construct aqueducts out of pieces of boards, sheets of tin and wires, always racing against time. A long team of workers snakes its way across the landscape. Picks rise and fall in unison. Spades burrow and pile the dirt and stones. Rocks are yanked out by hand. When the trench is complete in its tortuous, two-mile course over the jagged hillsides, the men cut the final few feet into the bank of the stream. The water gushes from the stream and courses along the ditch. At places where the water spills over the curves in the ditch, men throw themselves down and use their bodies as diversions. Finally the water spills into the fields, and people jump for joy in its muddy path.

The effectiveness of the irrigation ditch sequence is pure cinema. It seems a primitive device, but it was actually achieved with a great deal of artifice. Men could not have worked that fast or with that unity in actual fact, but it was Vidor's skill that made it look natural as well as exciting. He choreographed the sequence with the use of a metronome and thereby gave it visual rhythms. He used a bass drum to follow the beats of the metronome set to 4/4 time. The picks came down on the beats of one and three, and the shovels dug into the dirt on the count of two and pitched the dirt on the count of four. As the ditch neared completion Vidor increased the tempo slightly and heightened the excitement with each shot. Later, composer Alfred Newman was able to utilize Vidor's musical construction for even better effect.

The digging of the ditch was supposed to be done in two or three days according to the script, but in fact it took Vidor and his workers ten days. But film is illusion, and Vidor was able with his musical sense and a slight increasing of camera speeds to create a sequence that was fully convincing in its apparent reality. The mere digging of a ditch is far from exciting; it is to Vidor's credit that this particular ditch dig produces an emotional wallop.

In making the film Vidor rallied his cast and his extras with the same kind of enthusiasm that appeared on the screen in the making of the co-op. He was able to hire only two name players, Karen Morley and Tom Keene. She had done well in her film career, but Keene was known only as a star of cowboy pictures, and despite his success here he went back to his westerns. Vidor hired a large number of unemployed people in Los Angeles, together with a handful of professional actors, and was pleased to find them entering into the spirit of the story and pulling together in the manner of the characters in the script. The film brought in some conflicting reactions. It won a Russian prize, accompanied with a comment that the prize would have been bigger had not Vidor expressed his approval of capitalist propaganda in the spirit of the film. On the other hand some American critics, particularly those with the Hearst press,

John Qualen, Morley, and Keene.

A song-and-dance number: the co-op provides its own nightly entertainment.

The classic ditch-digging scene.

Frank Craven as the narrator of Our Town.

slapped Vidor for sympathizing with communist ideals and leaning toward the Left.

Our Daily Bread actually espouses no political view. It depicts people pulling together for their common good, and it is an accurate document of Americana, circa 1934. Vidor was able to bring in this remarkable and unusual film on his small budget and took pride when it received a League of Nations award for humanitarianism. Says Vidor, "When the completed film was shown, it was well received by the critics. Nor did it do badly at the box office. Nobody lost any money on the venture; we were well compensated by a fair return for our efforts, and by the greater satisfaction of having turned out a film which was true to our intentions and faithfully depicted our times."

William Holden and Martha Scott,
the young lovers of Our Town.

Sol Lesser, who died in 1980 at the age of eighty, had a long and profitable track record as a producer. Few of his films drew critical notices, indeed Lesser devoted much of his efforts to program product such as westerns and Tarzan adventures. But to Sol Lesser goes the credit for bringing to the screen one of the few genuine pieces of filmed Americana – Our Town. Hollywood has seldom, either before or after this fine film, shown much interest in turning literary or stage accounts of small-town life into movies and retaining their authenticity. Our Town is a shining exception. Lesser acquired the rights to Thornton Wilder's Pulitzer Prize-winning play, which opened on Broadway in the winter of 1938, and hired the author to work on the screenplay, assuring him that the film would retain the spirit of the play and, as nearly as possible, the script of the play. Lesser felt that the unusual play should be an unusual film. Wilder had

broken new ground in the American theatre with the concept of Our Town, which called for simplicity in its sets and scenery, and its use of an on-stage narrator to tell the story of two families in the New Hampshire village of Grovers Corners during the early years of the century. Frank Craven, the actor who had played the narrator in the original stage production, was hired not only to repeat his role for the film but to work with Harry Chandlee on writing the screenplay. And Thornton Wilder was consulted at every step.

Our Town is about as atypical a Hollywood film of 1940 as could be imagined. This applies even to its score. Lesser wisely turned to Aaron Copland, rather than the veteran Hollywood composers, to write music that would be in keeping with the gentle nature of Wilder's play. The result was music of lighter texture than the usual scoring practices of the time. It calls for a

29

Beulah Bondi and Fay Bainter, the two mothers.

Holden and Thomas Mitchell, the son and father.

Mitchell and Bainter.

small orchestra, with simple themes and a soft, somewhat melancholy ambience, which is perfect for the film. To create his set Lesser called on the renowned William Cameron Menzies, whose credits included the recent *Gone With the Wind*, and for his director Lesser chose Sam Wood, who by 1940 had been in the business for twenty years and had just concluded a long contract with MGM, his final item for them being *Goodbye, Mr. Chips.* For his cast he picked such tried and true performers as Thomas Mitchell, Fay Bainter, Beulah Bondi, and Guy Kibbee, and for his attractive young leads he chose twenty-two-year-old William Holden, who had made his debut the previous year in the aptly titled *Golden Boy*, and Martha Scott, who had not appeared on film before but who had played the part on Broadway.

Mr. Morgan (Craven) is the druggist in Grovers Corners, and he talks to the audience about his community and its people. Early one morning as the town is sleeping, he climbs a hill, stops by a rail fence, and remembers certain days. He recalls May seventh, 1901, because it was a typical, quiet, uneventful day but one which gave hints of changes coming up. The lights start coming on in the houses: Howie Newsome (Stuart Erwin), the milkman, and little Joe Crowell (Tim Davis), the newsboy, prepare to go about their rounds. Dr. Gibbs (Thomas Mitchell) arrives home after a night delivering a baby, and Mrs. Gibbs (Fay Bainter), always neat in her well-ironed gingham dress, prepares breakfast for him. He tells her it was twins and an easy delivery, then he tries to sleep for a couple of hours before his next patient is scheduled. Their son George (Holden) is crazy about baseball, and his father has to take him aside and point out that his mother is having to chop wood for the fireplace because George is spending a bit too much time with his baseball. George doesn't have to be told again.

Mr. Morgan thinks about the Webbs, who live next door to the Gibbs. Mr. Webb (Kibbee) is the editor of the town paper, the *Sentinel*, and he is still proud of the fact that his wife (Bondi) was once the prettiest girl in town. Their daughter Emily (Scott) is also pretty, and bright in school, too. So bright that she has to

The lovers marry.

help George with his homework, especially algebra, which George can't fathom. She and George walk home from school together every day, and he tells her he looks out his window every night and watches her as she does her homework. He tells her that he wants to be a farmer and that his uncle Luke will most likely give him a job and probably leave him the place in time. Then he remembers he has a baseball game to play and off he goes.

Five years pass and Mr. Morgan remembers that the baseball team is pretty upset. George is getting married to Emily and he is quitting the team. Howie Newsome has to deliver a lot of milk and cream that day to the Webbs because they are expecting a houseful of relatives for the wedding. Mrs. Webb starts to cry when she realizes that Emily is sitting down to breakfast for the last time, and Emily cries, too. The Gibbs are not feeling all that happy either. Mrs. Gibbs wonders how George will ever get along without her to arrange his clothes and see that he dresses warmly. He and Emily are so young. George starts to wish he was back at school and resents the way people are pushing him to grow older. But folks are meant to go through life two by two, so

Milkman Howie Newsome (Stuart Erwin) greets editor Webb (Guy Kibbee).

they say, and when George sees Emily at the church, so lovely in her wedding gown, all his doubts vanish. They make one of the most handsome couples Grovers Corners has ever seen, and they are sure to be happy. To be happy is everything, so they say.

Now it's 1913 and as Mr. Morgan points out, things have changed in Grovers Corners. People, especially the young folks, want to go to the movies and dress like the city folks they see on the screen. And people are now starting to lock their doors. There hasn't been any crime in Grovers Corners, but they have heard about things in other places nearby. Better not to take any chances. George and Emily have fixed up their farm house very nicely, but a crisis has come into their lives. Emily is having her second baby and she is fighting for her life. In her delirium as she hovers between life and death Emily imagines strange things. The past becomes the present and the dead seem to live again.

Emily imagines she sees so many who have gone – Mrs. Biggs, Joe the newspaper boy, and her brother Wallace, who died when his appendix burst while on a Boy Scout trip. And many others. In seeing the past Emily comes to love the present and all it has to offer, despite the troubles. How wonderful the earth is – why don't the living realize that? How troubled people are! How blind they are to the preciousness of life! Then Emily hears her new-born baby cry, and she is joyful to know she is alive and still part of life. As *Our Town* closes, Mr. Morgan says, "Eleven o'clock in Grovers Corners. Everybody's resting. Tomorrow's going to be another day. You get a good rest, too. Goodnight."

Our Town was not a box office champion in 1940. It was too radical a departure from conventional movies to draw crowds, but it did fairly well and easily covered its costs. More importantly it set a new standard in American cinema and showed the possibility of new kinds of film technique. The poignancy of the film does not diminish, and it gathers even more charm with time. It endures as a very special portrait of and contribution to American life. It was a courageous undertaking for Sol Lesser, and he had every reason to take pride in it, as did director Sam Wood, who captured the flavor of the small town. The acting is faultless, as are the contributions of designer Menzies, composer Copland, and photographer Bert Glennon.

In reviewing it for the *New York Times*, Bosley Crowther said: "We hesitate to employ superlatives but of *Our Town* the least we can say is that it captures on film the simple beauties and truths of humble folks as very few pictures ever do; it is rich and ennobling in its plain philosophy – and it gives one a passionate desire to enjoy the fullness of life even in these good old days of today."

Zachary Scott, title character of The Southerner.

The Southerner begins with the pages of an old album being turned and the voice of Tim (Charles Kemper) commenting: "This here is a little souvenir, a picture of my best pal, Sam Tucker, and his folks. Believe me, they don't come no better. When old Sam gets an idea in that hard head of his there ain't no room for nothin' else. This is Nona, Sam's wife. Here's Sam's Ma, widow woman. Not so young, but her heart's still full of fire. Harmie here ain't no Tucker, just a good friend. If he looks kind of sheep-eyed, it's 'cause he's all lit up with that flame in Ma's heart. These are the youngest of the Tucker clan…Sam's kids…Daisy and Jottie. And here's Sam's Granny. She didn't like havin' her picture taken neither. This one's me. I'm a town man myself. Only come home for burials, weddings and such. That's how I come to cherish these pictures so. Makes me feel close to my friends as I look at 'em."

The opening is true to the remainder of the film, which contains little in the way of plot but a lot in the way of character studies of simple farming people in East Texas, and which portrays them with compassion and accuracy. They are literally dirt poor, and *The Southerner* is perhaps the only Hollywood film to deal with this segment of American life in such an honest fashion. Perhaps there is a little irony in the fact that the film is not the work of an American director but a Frenchman reared in an atmosphere of great art. Jean Renoir, the son of the legendary painter Auguste Renoir, made a name for himself in the late thirties as a director, particularly for *La Grande Illusion* (1937). He came to California in 1940, after the German occupation of France, and stayed for the duration of the war. His first American film was *Swamp Water*, a drama set among the Georgia backwaters, followed by *This Land Is Mine* (1943), a story of occupied France, and then *The Southerner*. After that Renoir would make two more American pictures – *Diary of a Chambermaid* (1945) and *The Woman on the Beach* (1947) – before returning to France. None of his American efforts were greatly successful in terms of income, but they were all interesting and admired pieces of film making, especially *The Southerner*.

The Southerner is gentle, unpretentious, and honest, but it received some adverse publicity when first released. The censors in Memphis, Tennessee, banned it because it presented southerners as "illiterate mendicants." It met with similar grunts of disapproval in other places in the South but no other outright bannings. The critical reaction elsewhere was high, and the film easily earned back its investment, although there was no likelihood of it ever being a box office smash. The "illiterate mendicants" to whom the people in Memphis referred are a

Scott, Jay Gilpin, and Betty Field: the family goes fishing.

Scott, Field, Bunny Sunshine, Jay Gilpin, and
Beulah Bondi: the family at home.

family of sharecroppers – Sam Tucker (Zachary Scott), his wife Nona (Betty Field), their two small children, Daisy (Bunny Sunshine) and Jot (Jay Gilpin), and Sam's crotchety old Granny (Beulah Bondi) – who wrestle a meager living from a sadly deficient strip of land in the flood plain of a treacherous Texas river. The story takes place during the course of a year, which starts with the Tuckers giving up their migratory field work as cotton pickers and settling down as tenants on a piece of land, on which they plant their first crop of cotton. They get the derelict house into shape and take pleasure in having a home, but they find little in the way of charity, either from the soil or from their nearest neighbor, Devers (J. Carrol Naish), a man so embittered by poverty that there is no room in his heart for helping anyone else. Their son Jot falls ill with what they call "spring sickness."

However the visiting doctor, who refuses to take what little money they have – a couple of dollars – advises them the boy has pellagra and needs vegetables and milk. They plant a vegetable garden, but when they approach Devers for some milk he tells them he cannot spare any, even as he tips a bucket of milk into a pig's trough. A short while later the Tuckers wake up to find their vegetable garden demolished by Devers's hogs, at which Sam goes to Devers and beats him in a savage fist fight. Devers then goes after Sam with his rifle and catches up to him at the river. But there fate brings them together. A giant catfish Devers has been trying to catch for months surfaces and with Sam's help, Devers reels in the fish. After that the Tuckers have access to Devers's milk and vegetables.

Sam and Nona take pleasure in their first cotton crop, now

ready for picking, and one night go into the nearby town to attend the wedding of Sam's mother (Blanche Yurka) to their friend Harmie (Percy Kilbride), who runs the general store. Sam and his friends enjoy the fun and the drinking but at the end of the day it starts to rain, more and more heavily. Sam and Nona borrow a car and rush home. The heavy rains ruin their crop. Whines Granny, "Looks like a sow's nest." The land is devastated by the storm, and Sam gives thought to leaving it all and taking a job as a worker in a factory. But Nona still has hope. She straightens up the house, and Granny pulls out of her depression long enough to tell Sam that something like this happened to her and his grandfather forty-three years ago, and they survived. It occurs to Sam that he has been wrong in planting only cotton, but that he should try potatoes and corn and beans, "L'il bit o' everythin'." Life goes on.

Few American directors have looked as closely at grassroots America as did Jean Renoir in this fine film. Perhaps it takes an artist from another country to spot qualities and characteristics that might miss the eye of the native, such things as the pleasure a family has in lighting their first fire in a home, of cooking and eating meat that the head of the family has himself hunted, and of seeing the results of work done with backs and hands – and the anguish of having it all subject to the spasms of nature.

The Southerner barely came into being. Renoir and his producers, David Loew and Robert Hakim, were able to get a distribution contract from United Artists on the basis of an

On location: director Jean Renoir is the stout gentleman, with white shirt and large fedora, sitting on the camera platform.

The couple after the storm.

Kilbride and Blanche Yurka with Scott and Field.

agreement from Joel McCrea and his wife Frances Dee to star in the film. But when McCrea saw the script he decided it was not the kind of material he could handle and United Artists withdrew the contract, on which basis the producers had sought their backing. David Loew then told United Artists that unless they agreed to handle *The Southerner* he would not release any of his further productions through them. At that they reluctantly changed their stand and gave Renoir his distribution contract. Loew asked Renoir which actor he would like to play the lead, and Renoir picked Zachary Scott, who had made a recent successful movie debut in *The Mask of Dimitrios*, in which he played a sophisticated gangster. Renoir always liked to pick actors who were not obvious choices, reasoning that it made the roles more interesting and gave the actor more of a challenge. However, in the case of the usually dapper Scott, Renoir was well aware that the actor was a Texan and could handle the accent perfectly.

Renoir's desire to film on the actual locations of the story, in Texas, was frustrated by wartime travel restrictions and by the film's modest budget. A good substitute location was found in California's San Joaquin Valley, near the town of Madera, where cotton is grown, and Renoir's set designer Eugene Lourié took an apparent delight in the challenge of building a tumbledown shack. In his book *My Life and My Films* Renoir said: "What attracted me in the story was precisely the fact that there was really no story, nothing but a series of strong impressions – the vast landscape, the simple aspiration of the hero, the heat and the hunger. Being forced to live a life restricted to their daily material needs, the characters attain a level of spirituality of which they themselves are unaware." That level of folksy spirituality is apparent in *The Southerner*, as it must be in all worthwhile films dealing with grassroots America.

39

Walter Brennan and Gary Cooper: hobos camping under the bridge.

(Left)
Frank Capra and James Stewart.

TWO

CAPRACORN

The word "Capracorn" is one coined by Frank Capra himself, and it can only be taken as a flippant reference to his own tendency toward an idealistic approach to the American experience. It is not a word used disparagingly. Capra's America is certainly not the America of today – unfortunately – and his optimistic attitudes would be at variance with current filmic accounts of American life. The value of his views, aside from the pure skill of his craft and his ability to tell a story, is the proof he offers of the good life. Despite the moral decline and chaos of recent American years, it is impossible to watch Gary Cooper in *Meet John Doe* or James Stewart in *It's a Wonderful Life* and not be impressed with the beauty of common virtues. The message is clear. Forget what life *is* – look at Capra and see what life *should* be. And in projecting images of ideal male Americana, Capra never found two more perfect specimens than James Stewart and Gary Cooper.

Possibly no actor personified the American Everyman better than Gary Cooper. He was an idealization of the way Americans like to see themselves – honest, straightforward, likable, and devoid of intellectual and social conceits. He was quiet and strong, and as such he appealed to men as well as women. On the legitimate stage he would probably have been lost, but on the screen he had a magic presence. John Barrymore once said of Cooper, "He can do, with no effort, what the rest of us spent

Cooper and Barbara Stanwyck.

years trying to learn – to be perfectly natural." Charles Laughton, who starred with Cooper in *The Devil and the Deep* (1932), thought that Cooper himself did not realize how talented an actor he was. Certainly Cooper could never verbalize about the art of acting, but his friend Robert Preston said, after Cooper died, "He was probably the finest motion picture actor I ever worked with."

Although he often played cowboys and men of little education, Cooper actually experienced some contact with the higher levels of society. He was born in Montana in 1901, but his parents were British and his father, who was a state supreme court judge, sent the boy to England to finish his schooling at Dunstable, where the father had received his own education. With the outbreak of war in 1914 Cooper returned to Montana and was later enrolled in Wesleyan College in Bozeman, Montana, where he developed his flair as an artist. His cartoons and caricatures started to appear in print when he attended Grinnell College in Iowa, in both the school magazine and Cooper's hometown paper, the *Helena Independent.* During the summers he worked as a guide at Yellowstone National Park. In previous summers and on many weekends, Cooper had worked on his father's ranch and there learned a lot about the job of being a cowboy, a knowledge that would soon be of great advantage to him.

When Cooper Senior retired from the bench, he and his wife went to live in San Diego, California. Gary visited them in late 1924 and decided to remain in the state and try to find work as a newspaper artist. He failed to get any assignments but during Christmas of that year he ran into some Montana friends in Los Angeles and found they were making a living as extras in western

Cooper being groomed as John Doe with newspapermen Pat Flaherty, Irving Bacon, Warren Hymer, and Hank Mann scrutinizing him.

movies. They received ten dollars a day for riding around on horses and more if they did simple stunts – like falling off. They introduced Cooper to various casting directors and from then on Gary Cooper was part of the picture business. He appeared in countless westerns during 1925, and the following year, with the help of an agent who believed in his potential, Cooper was given a small part in *The Winning of Barbara Worth*, starring Ronald Colman and Vilma Banky. Producer Samuel Goldwyn offered him $65 a week to stay on, but the agent didn't think it was enough and got Cooper $150 a week at Paramount, which soon signed him to a long term contract. By 1930, with films like *The Spoilers* and *Morocco*, he was a star, and a star he remained for the rest of his life.

In 1936 Frank Capra arranged for Cooper to be loaned to Columbia to star in his *Mr. Deeds Goes to Town*, the story of a bashful small-town young man who inherits twenty million dollars and gives it away. The film brought Capra an Oscar, and Cooper received his first nomination. From then on Capra and his writer-collaborator Robert Riskin determined to find another vehicle for Cooper. It came about one day in November of 1939 when a writer friend, Robert Presnell, handed Capra a story he had written with Robert Connell called *The Life and Death of John Doe*. Capra read it in an hour and immediately bought it. He had only one man in mind for John Doe and that was Gary Cooper. He phoned Cooper and described the story but explained that he did not yet have a script. Replied Cooper, "It's okay, Frank. I don't need a script."

Meet John Doe was Capra's first independent production. It was made under an agreement with Warner Bros., who would be responsible for some of the production costs and the

Edward Arnold threatens Cooper for rebelling against his scheme, while henchman Rod La Rocque looks on.

distribution. But Capra had complete artistic control, and Warners gave no interference in his intended attack on incipient fascism in America. The story is about a former baseball player named Long John Willoughby (Cooper) who has been reduced to the hobo level by an injury to his pitching arm. A newspaper columnist, Ann Mitchell (Barbara Stanwyck), spots him and brings him to the office of her editor (James Gleason) because she needs a man to fill the image of her invented character, John Doe. Ann has written a story attacking government hypocrisy and business corruption, and signed it with the name John Doe. It further declares that the writer will commit suicide on Christmas Eve as a way of protesting the hypocrisy and corruption. Rival newspapers claim the letter is a publicity hoax, and owner D.B. Norton (Edward Arnold) demands that Ann find a man who will fill the role of moral crusader. The hungry, penniless Long John

agrees to take the job, and the response from the public is so strong that the newspaper prints a whole series of articles by John Doe, although actually written by Ann. Circulation increases as he points out all the injustices heaped upon the workers of the land, the common folk, who respond by setting up John Doe clubs and giving him their support. Mail floods the newspaper offices, and John's popularity leaps when he starts doing a daily radio broadcast.

D.B. Norton encourages the public following because he intends to use it for his own political purposes. He is not content with being a wealthy baron of business, with his own uniformed police force; he wants to become president of the United States as the leader of his own third party. Ann, who is now in love with the honest and incorruptible John Doe, realizes she has created a dangerous situation. Norton calls for a national convention of

The final rebellion at the political rally.

all the John Doe clubs. At the massive gathering Norton rallies the crowd and tells them of his plans for the country, all of them in line with the sentiments laid down by their beloved John Doe. But when John arrives to tell the crowd what he has already told Norton – that Norton is a fraud and a fascist – Norton cuts the microphone lines. John fails to make himself heard to the followers, who turn away from him in disgust when Norton denounces him as a fake.

John Doe reasons that the only way to prove to his public that he is not a fake is to keep the pledge made in the original letter – to commit suicide on Christmas Eve by leaping from the top of the city hall. Norton and his group are there on the cold snowy night and so is Ann and some of the faithful followers of John Doe. Ann, contrite at the situation she has put him in and deeply in love with him, pleads with him not to kill himself, that it will serve no good purpose and that it is better to live and fight the Nortons of the world. She faints and John picks her up. As he walks toward his supporters he turns and says, "There you are,

Norton – the people. Try and lick that."

Only the ending of this fine movie rings slightly false, but after five different versions Capra and Riskin decided it was the best. Most of the picture, and all of the acting, is superb, particularly Cooper's. Said Howard Barnes in the *New York Herald Tribune*: "The part was hand tailored for the actor but he does more than just fit it. He gives a splendid and utterly persuasive portrayal.... Only Cooper, I believe, could have so completely fulfilled Capra's conception in *Meet John Doe*." It would doubtless have brought him an Oscar nomination but for the stiff competition Cooper gave himself. A few months after the Capra picture was released Cooper appeared in *Sergeant York*. The public liked him in that one even more, and it was *Sergeant York* that brought him his first Oscar. Eleven years later he won another, for *High Noon*. But the winning of two Oscars are minor factors when matched with the value of the overall body of Cooper's work and his enduring image in film history.

High school dance from It's a Wonderful Life.

W. S. Van Dyke, who directed James Stewart in three films, once described the actor as being "unusually usual," which is about as good a description as any of a man who has become one of the classic figures of the American screen by espousing homey virtues and appearing to be ordinary. He is, of course, an extraordinary man, and the seventy movies in which he has starred over a more than forty-year period are a testament to his deceptive skill. Stewart has always appeared to be at ease in front of the cameras, to be natural, and to be himself. But as any actor knows, these qualities come only with exceptional ability.

James Stewart was born in May of 1908 in a Pennsylvania town called Indiana. His father ran a hardware business that had

Scenes from
It's a Wonderful Life.

48

been founded a generation before. As a boy he showed ability with mechanical construction, which led him to apply for a course in civil engineering when he enrolled at Princeton University. He had no thoughts about being an actor, but he did enjoy playing the accordion, and it was this talent that brought him into the theatrical presentations of Princeton's celebrated Triangle Club. One of the most prominent members was Joshua Logan, who became one of the directors of the summer theatre at Falmouth, Massachusetts, after he left Princeton. After Stewart's graduation he was hired by Logan as an accordionist and was soon encouraged by Logan to take bit parts in his productions. Stewart found that he liked acting and decided to make it his career.

In the fall of 1932 Stewart and a group of the Falmouth actors, including Henry Fonda, went to New York and roomed together as they looked for work. Stewart was lucky, partly because the Falmouth influence on Broadway was good, and got a part in *Carrie Nation*, as did Joshua Logan. Over the next two years he appeared in a half dozen other plays and always received good notices. Of his performance in *Yellow Jack*, critic Robert Garland of the *World Telegram* said, "It is simple, sensitive and true. And replete with poetic underbeat." In late 1934 he was cast as Judith Anderson's son in *Divided by Two*, which ran for only thirty-one performances but proved to be the turning point in his life. One of the other performers in the play was Hedda Hopper, who praised his work when she returned to Hollywood and suggested to MGM that they take a look at him. They did. They gave him a screen test and brought him to the studio in Culver City – and the morning he turned up for work he was assigned to a small part in the Spencer Tracy crime picture *Murder Man*. His stock soared shortly afterwards when Margaret Sullivan, who had played opposite him in several Falmouth productions, requested him for the role of her husband in *Next Time We Love*, which required MGM to loan him to Universal. His success in the Sullivan picture moved MGM to find plenty of work for him when he returned to the home studio. Within a couple of years Stewart was a Name, especially when Frank Capra borrowed him in 1938 for *You Can't Take It With You* at Columbia, and then borrowed him again a year later for *Mr. Smith Goes to Washington*.

Stewart won an Oscar for his role as the sly reporter in *The Philadelphia Story* and then, after three more films, his career was severely interrupted. He was drafted – and became the first major Hollywood personality to enter the armed forces prior to

Scenes from
It's a Wonderful Life.

America's entry into the war. He joined the army in March of 1941, and because of his interest in flying – he had logged four hundred hours as a civilian pilot – he was attached to the air corps. After a half-year as a mechanic he was commissioned and made an instructor. War brought promotion and by the middle of 1943 Stewart was a Lieutenant Colonel, stationed in England with the Eighth Air Corps and in command of a squadron of B-24 bombers. His services brought him a number of decorations, including the Croix de Guerre and the Distinguished Flying Cross with Oak Leaf Cluster. After the war he remained with the Air Force Reserve, and by the time he retired in 1970 he had reached the rank of Brigadier General.

Stewart's contract with MGM lapsed during the years he was in the service and when he returned to Hollywood he was welcomed with open arms by Louis B. Mayer, who was astonished when the actor declined. He agreed to make films for them, but he wanted no more long-term contracts. Like other stars who had returned from the war he was a more mature man, and he felt the need for different and better pictures and, more

importantly, to dictate the course and terms of his career.

Frank Capra returned to Hollywood at about the same time. He, too, had been in the army, not as a warrior but as a director of documentary films, and the first film he wanted to make on his return was *It's a Wonderful Life*, the title of which accurately reveals Capra's optimism and vigor. Even before he had the script written he visited James Stewart in order to get him for the lead. Stewart listened to Capra's rather confusing yarn about a man who wants to kill himself but is prevented from so doing by his guardian angel. After a while he just stopped Capra and said, yes, he'd be delighted to play the part.

It's a Wonderful Life is a rosy-eyed view of the human condition. One critic suggested it be listed right next to Dickens's *A Christmas Carol* for its attempts to persuade the audience that all is well, eventually. Here Stewart is George Bailey, who leads what he thinks is a pretty dull life in the small town of Bedford Falls, running his father's building and loan company. When his father (Samuel S. Hinds) dies, George takes over and finds that a great many people in the town have leaned heavily on his father's easy-

going ways. But George is the same kind of man, which means that cash-flow is low, and the prospects of keeping the company afloat are slim. In desperation he turns to the town's principal banker, Henry Potter (Lionel Barrymore), for a loan. Since Potter has planned to ruin George and to have the entire business of Bedford Falls at his command, he does nothing to help.

The only really good thing in George's life, as he sees it, is his marriage to Mary (Donna Reed), although he feels badly that he has never been able to keep his promise to take her traveling around the world. When his uncle (Thomas Mitchell) accidentally loses the company funds, George is faced with ruin. It seems his generosity has been his undoing. One dark and snowy night he stands on the town bridge and tells himself he wishes he had never been born. Before George has a chance to jump, an old fellow named Clarence Oddbody (Henry Travers) throws himself in the river in order to be saved by George. Later he tells George that he is his guardian angel and that before he kills

himself he ought to take a look at Bedford Falls and what it would be like if he had never lived. It would be, he sees, a different and far less nice place to live. The cold-hearted, despotic Potter would run everything, and George's many friends would be leading rather dismal lives. After seeing this side of the picture, George is eager to be back in the land of the living. Returning to his home he finds his friends have rallied on his behalf and collected enough money to stop his business from falling into Potter's hands. Life, George realizes, is indeed wonderful.

Capra's glowingly optimistic *It's a Wonderful Life* seemed somewhat at variance with the postwar spirit, and it failed to make a big noise at the box office windows. But distance has lent it enchantment. Among film makers it is regarded as a masterpiece, and wherever it is shown today audiences respond to it as a beautiful evocation of former American values – with the hope that they are not gone forever. And much of the impact of the picture is due, as Capra is the first to point out, to the remarkable James Stewart.

Grandmother (May Robson), friend (Andy Devine), and studio chief (Adolphe Menjou) attend the premiere of Vicki Lester's new picture.

(Left)
Janet Gaynor as Vicki Lester winning the Oscar in A Star Is Born.

THREE

ILLUSION AND THE TOUCH OF CLASS

Film is illusion. It can never be anything else. Despite all the efforts to project realism, the final result is still illusion. Once something is photographed and projected on a screen it becomes something else. Truth on film is a very subjective kind of truth, always at the mercy of those who make the film. The danger lies in the fact that film *looks* like reality. It is therefore possible to watch Fred Astaire and assume that because he is a nice, ordinary looking kind of fellow, his dancing is therefore something that he does easily and naturally. That is truly illusion. Hundreds of hours of painstaking development and rehearsal go into an Astaire dance, as do many hours of shooting and even more hours of editing. Astaire is totally *extraordinary*. So too are the best actors, like William Powell and Fredric March, no matter how smooth and gentlemanly they appear on screen. What distinguishes the work of Astaire, March, and Powell is quality. They are gentlemen with *class*, and they give class to the films in which they appear. It is Astaire's class that allows the audience to accept him as an average college boy in *Second Chorus* and Powell as a butler in *My Man Godfrey*. It

surely is class which allowed March to give credence to the opportunistic reporter in *Nothing Sacred* and to the alcoholic movie star in that almost accurate portrayal of Hollywood, *A Star Is Born*.

Americans have always tended to play down the business of personal classiness. It is a country founded on the virtues of the common man, and even though the concept of free enterprise encourages people to gain the better life, Americans expect their leaders to remain common people, albeit with dignity and a little style. It was, after all, a country created in a deliberate breakaway from the brutal strictures of European class distinctions. But class will out, and Americans still look somewhat

wistfully at the better examples of European royalty and the dignity of truly decent upper-crust men and women. The need to idolize and admire has not escaped Americans any more than it has people of other countries, and that need has been met by the movies. The stars of Hollywood, especially in that Golden Age, were the American royalty. The public was able to select its own aristocracy – the beautiful, the heroic, the amusing, and the classy stylists.

The art of being a gentleman has somewhat fallen out of favor in today's movie market, which is not surprising in view of worldwide cynicism and despair, but the desire to identify with a dancer like Fred Astaire is never likely to diminish. Astaire is refined of manner, but he is not snooty and distant as might be a great artist in another country. He is, seemingly, a *nice guy* and he is an American. And wouldn't it be wonderful to be able to dance like him? Bing Crosby often said his success came from his ability to make people think that he was not all that great and that with a little luck almost anybody could sing as well. In other words, we all sound like Bing in the shower and dance like Fred in our dreams. It is, of course, entirely a matter of classy illusion, and it stems entirely from the art of the people who make movies. What distinguishes and separates American movie illusion from that of other lands is that Hollywood has always been aware of American values and has successfully merchandised them. In no other country has a form of entertainment been so aware of national idealism and supported the concept of the way a people would like to see themselves. Again, this pertains more to the past than the present, but only a total pessimist is likely to give up the ghost. There is still plenty of evidence of idealism in America even though it seldom appears on the contemporary screen. Those who are distressed by the brutality and negativism in current movies had best remind themselves that it is possibly no more true than the rosy pictures of the past. Accuracy has never been a factor in commercial movie making in California.

If Hollywood chose not to give an accurate picture of America during those years of the Golden Era, it was even less concerned in portraying itself with any verisimilitude. Indeed, the tendency was more in the other direction; whatever notions the public had about Hollywood, about its supposed allure, its romantic and scandalous fables, were capitalized upon in the movies about the movies. For largely comedic purposes Hollywood turned the cameras on itself to reveal egocentric actors, venal producers, eccentric directors, neurotic writers, and hustling agents. Of the more than two hundred features the industry had made about itself, few have taken a deeply serious look at the hard facts of life in Hollywood and the tough nature of the film industry. Only a handful of these films, such as *Sunset Boulevard* (1950), *Singin' in the Rain* (1952), *The Bad and the Beautiful* (1952), *The Big Knife* (1955), and *The Goddess* (1958), can be regarded as first-rate movies. But high on that list stands David O. Selznick's 1937 version of *A Star Is Born*, with Fredric March as the alcoholic movie star whose career is on the wane and Janet Gaynor as the young actress who marries him and ascends to stardom. It was remade in 1954 with Judy Garland and James Mason, and in 1976 with Barbra Streisand and Kris Kristofferson, but neither gave quite as much insight into the ways and means of Hollywood as did the Selznick version.

In 1932 Selznick, in a resolve to make a good film about Hollywood, commissioned writer Adela Rogers St. Johns to put together a script that would show some of the hardships involved in pursuing stardom and the often high emotional costs in maintaining it. The result was *What Price Hollywood?* starring Constance Bennett as a girl who makes good and Lowell Sherman as the alcoholic director who helps her but who cannot save his own career, and commits suicide. Mrs. St. Johns claimed that her characters were composites of people she had known. The film did well, and five years later Selznick decided to expand the idea and spend more money for an even more ambitious look at the heart of the picture business. This brought about *A Star Is Born*, a story concept that was given to him by William Wellman, who was then hired to direct it. For the part of Vicki Lester, the girl who strikes it lucky and becomes a star, Selznick chose Janet Gaynor, a star whose own popularity was actually on the decline, and for Norman Maine, the matinee idol on the way down, he picked Fredric March, a star whose career was very much on the way up. March had won an Oscar in 1932 for *Dr. Jekyll and Mr. Hyde*, and his gentlemanly private life and his professional prestige could hardly have been more removed from the image of the weak, hedonistic Norman Maine.

Norman Maine was a composite of the flamboyant manner of alcoholic John Barrymore, the charmingly mercurial John Gilbert, whose career plummeted with the coming of sound, and John Bowers, an actor who had enjoyed a spurt of popularity but who by 1936 had been out of work for some years. Separated from his actress wife Marguerite de la Motte, Bowers one night rowed out into the Pacific in a small boat. The next day his body was washed up on the shore. No such dramatic inspiration was needed to create the role of Vicki Lester – thousands of such girls turn up every year in Hollywood.

A Star Is Born begins with Esther Blodgett (Gaynor) having arrived at her Montana home after a visit to the movies and reminding her family that she wants to go to Hollywood and become an actress. Her grandmother (May Robson) is the only one who takes her at all seriously and loans her the bus fare. Esther proceeds to California and finds, as multitudes have already found before, that it is exceedingly difficult to get into the business. She is befriended by an assistant director (Andy Devine), and one evening they witness Norman Maine making a drunken nuisance of himself at the Hollywood Bowl. She next sees Maine when she is hired as a waitress for a party at the home of producer Oliver Niles (Adolphe Menjou). Bored with the guests, Maine wanders into the kitchen and there helps Esther

do some dishes, a number of which smash as he fumbles with the towel. To escape the notice created by the noise he takes her out of the house and for a ride in his car. He asks about her, and Esther tells him of her hopes to be an actress. Maine, sensing that she has a certain quality, offers to help and later bullies Niles into giving Esther a screen test. The test is successful, and Esther finds herself with a new name – Vicki Lester – and a chance to appear in a film with Maine. At the premiere the comments make it plain that she is a vital discovery and that Maine is a tired and fading name.

Despite warnings that she should now leave Maine, she reveals her love and gratitude by marrying him. They annoy Niles and his publicist (Lionel Stander) by shunning the glittering ceremony the studio plans to stage and slipping away to be married in a small town. Maine's career continues to deflate, and Vicki's soars to the heights. He makes a sad, drunken spectacle of himself when she receives an Academy Award and afterwards submits himself to a period in a sanitarium to cure his drinking.

The sad decline of Norman Maine.

He does well until the publicist, bitter because of past humiliations, snidely points out that Maine can now relax and live off his wife. He resorts to the bottle and ends up one evening in jail. Maine is released in Vicki's custody but a few days later he overhears a conversation in which he is described as a shell of his former self. He tells her he is a new man, and a sober one, but Maine realizes the burden he has become and makes the decision to end his life. He walks into the sea and drowns himself. His death is publicized as an accident, and the stricken Vicki opts for retiring from the screen. Her grandmother is among those who point out to her that Maine sacrificed himself so that he would not be a drawback to her career and that she owes it to him, herself, and her admirers to go on. Some time later she attends a film premiere, and when the announcer asks her to step up to the microphone, Vicki proudly says, "This is Mrs. Norman Maine…."

A Star Is Born strikes just the right balance between a warm regard for its protagonists and a cool look at the workings and character of the film industry. Selznick claimed that it was the fair assessment of Hollywood for which he has striven and that the dialogue was mostly "straight out of life and was straight 'reportage' so to speak." The film also showed a goodly amount of the actual functions of film making, including the grooming process for a novice about to take a screen test, and some now rather quaint shots of 1937 Los Angeles. It remains one of the best movies made about Hollywood. The 1954 remake is also excellent but the values of the film rest more heavily upon the characterizations than upon an examination of the nature of Hollywood. James Mason's finely etched version of Norman Maine is less sympathetic than March's – more dangerously capricious and with a meaner spirit – and Judy Garland's Vicki Lester is more complex and nervous than Gaynor's. Perhaps nostalgia lends enchantment to the view, but the Selznick original holds up as a touching love story and a finely detailed portrait of the Hollywood that used to be.

778-1

The heyday of American film comedy came in those years of Hollywood's general Golden Era – from the early thirties to the end of the Second World War. Once the screen had found a voice and had time to refine its verbal abilities, the result, thanks to an abundance of actors, writers, and directors, was a number of remarkably superior comedies, many of them in that strange category called *screwball*. The *screwball* comedy leaned more on wit than slapstick and usually dealt with people who were pleasingly eccentric and unpredictable. This was especially true of the Depression years, when Hollywood stressed an illusory concept of the American way of life. In his book *Lovers and Lunatics* Ted Sennett noted, "So many thirties comedies fostered and thrived on a double illusion: that poor families survived on charm, luck, and childlike innocence, while

rich families, lacking charm and needing no luck, frittered their time away with games, flirtations, and idle chatter. Poor families may have craved money but found life more cheerful without it. Rich families spent their money on frivolous pursuits but found that it couldn't buy love or happiness. A false dichotomy at best, it faded with the forties and the melding of the rich and poor in a common cause. But while it lasted, it formed the foundation for some enjoyable movies."

Of the kind of film to which Sennett referred, few equal the wit and sting of *My Man Godfrey*, where the contrast between wealth and poverty provides laughter while digging into social consciousness. Only the elegance of its performers and the taste of director Gregory La Cava hold the film back from crossing the line into bitter comment. The title character is Godfrey (William

Godfrey meets the upper crust and views them with mild contempt: Gail Patrick, Alice Brady, Carole Lombard, and Powell.

Powell), a derelict of gentlemanly demeanor who is first seen standing by an open fire in a New York City garbage dump. He is approached by a group of well-dressed people who offer him five dollars if he will do something for them. They are having a party and need a forgotten man (a Depression term for derelict) to complete a game they are playing. The game involves a scavenger hunt in which they must turn in a list of odd things in order to win. Godfrey is offended and pushes one of them, Cornelia (Gail Patrick) into a pile of ashes, which amuses her sister Irene (Carole Lombard), who says she has long wanted to do that to the arrogant Cornelia. Irene is much more appealing and manages to arouse Godfrey's curiosity. He goes to the party and after surveying the guests tells them, "My purpose in coming here tonight was two-fold. Firstly, I wanted to aid this young woman. Secondly, I was curious to see how a bunch of empty-headed nitwits conducted themselves."

Despite Godfrey's disgust, Irene charms him into accepting the job of butler to her family, the Bullocks, whom he quickly finds are mostly nitwits, divorced from the reality of the times. Mr. Bullock (Eugene Pallette) is sane and looks upon his dithery wife (Alice Brady) and his daughters in the same disdainful light as his new butler. Furthermore, their irresponsible ways with money are causing him to go broke. Godfrey is an excellent butler. He is disliked by Cornelia because she cannot cause a flutter in his calm, superior manner, and he is loved by Irene, who looks upon him as her protégé. Mr. Bullock is constantly appalled at the behavior of his daughters and constantly being served with subpoenas because of them. Godfrey takes pity and aids Bullock on the stock market, although Bullock does not know it. But it saves him from going broke. When Cornelia spitefully makes unkind inferences about Godfrey, her mother warns, "You mustn't come between Irene and Godfrey. He's the only thing she's shown any affection for since her Pomeranian died last summer." Godfrey does his best to cool Irene's ardor, but it does no good. She comes to adore him more and more.

A Bostonian friend of the family, Tommy Gray (Alan Mowbray), drops in on them and recognizes their butler as a fellow Harvard graduate, but at Godfrey's urging he keeps the information to himself. Godfrey, it seems, is a product of one of the upper-crust Boston families. Due to an unhappy love affair he drifted into despondency and considered suicide, but held back from throwing himself into the Hudson River when he saw the plight of men with genuinely tragic circumstances, and decided instead to join them in their makeshift camp in the city dump. Tommy agrees to keep Godfrey's secret and even claims that he once hired him as a butler himself, and found his services quite satisfactory. He also does as Godfrey asks and tells the Bullocks of his family of five children and an Indian wife, a ruse in order to ward off Irene's amorous interest.

Irene, annoyed at Godfrey's disclosure of family, announces her engagement to one of her socialite friends but bursts into tears when asked who he is. Says her father to Godfrey, "I sometimes wonder if my whole family has gone mad or whether it's me." Consoles Godfrey, "I know how you feel, sir. I've felt that way many times since I've been here," to which Bullock replies, "Then why do you stay here? I have to – you don't." Godfrey tells him he has pride in being a good butler and that it is better than living in a packing box on the city dump. Godfrey later returns to the dump with Tommy and points out various men who have hung onto life despite their misfortunes. He points out one man who was a bank president and went broke trying to see his depositors would not lose their savings. Tommy feels that Godfrey has a peculiar sense of humor in involving himself with men who are not his responsibility. Godfrey responds, "Over here we have some very fashionable apartment houses – over there is a swanky nightclub, while down here men starve for want of a job. How does that strike your sense of humor?"

Irene goes on a European trip to recover from her latest broken engagement, but it does nothing to cure her love for Godfrey. He tells her he is grateful to her for helping him get back into the business of being a functioning human being again but that it isn't reason enough for him to fall in love with her. He admits that all the talk about him having an Indian wife and a

Godfrey's transformation into a butler.

family was nonsense, which makes Irene very happy, but then tells her it is time for him to move on, which makes her very unhappy. She faints and he carries her to her room, where he quickly brings her to her senses by sticking her in the shower. But she merely accepts this as a token of his love and then runs around the house yelling, "Godfrey loves me!" Eventually Godfrey's identity is revealed by the always snooping Cornelia. Bullock tells his family he is broke, but Godfrey comes forth with the documents that show Bullock is not, explaining, "There comes a turning point in every man's life – a time when he needs help. It happened to me…" He goes on to explain that he has used some of the funds he earned by manipulating Bullock stock to promote a scheme to assist his underprivileged friends. Even Cornelia is impressed, especially when Godfrey thanks her for pointing out that it was her own bad example that taught him about humility and false pride: "Miss Cornelia, there have been other spoiled children in the world. I happened to be one of them myself. You're a high-spirited girl. I can only hope that you'll use those high spirits in a more constructive way. And so – good day."

Love will find a way, even in the kitchen: Lombard and Powell.

62

On the set with Brady, Lombard, Mischa Auer, Powell, and director Gregory La Cava.

There is now no stopping Irene in her pursuit of Godfrey. She turns up at the former site of the dump, which Godfrey has turned into a work project for his derelict friends. She takes advantage of the mayor being on hand and asks him if he is allowed to marry people without a license. He says that since he knows her family so well he can take a chance. "Who are you going to marry?" The amazed Godfrey is astounded to hear that he is the party in question. The mayor asks her if her father knows about this, and Irene replies, "Everybody knows about it except Godfrey." The mayor tells them to hold hands. She grabs his hand and tells him, "Stand still, Godfrey, it'll all be over in a minute."

My Man Godfrey does not lose its impact with the passing of time. Instead, it remains a textbook example of high comedic style. The script by Morrie Ryskind and Eric Hatch, and the performance of its cast make it permanently brilliant. William Powell could not be improved upon, Carole Lombard sparkles as the spoiled girl with a truly warm heart, and a word must be spoken for Eugene Pallette. Stocky, stout as a barrel, and with a voice like a foghorn he was often cast as an angry victim of other people's folly, a bewildered item of sanity bobbling in a sea of idiots. As Alexander Bullock, Pallette was at the peak of his form. He was one of the many superb American character actors who gave firm support to the facade of Hollywood.

Nothing Sacred: New York reporter Wally Cook (Fredric March) arrives in Warsaw, Vermont.

March trying to persuade his editor (Walter Connolly) to let him cover the story.

64

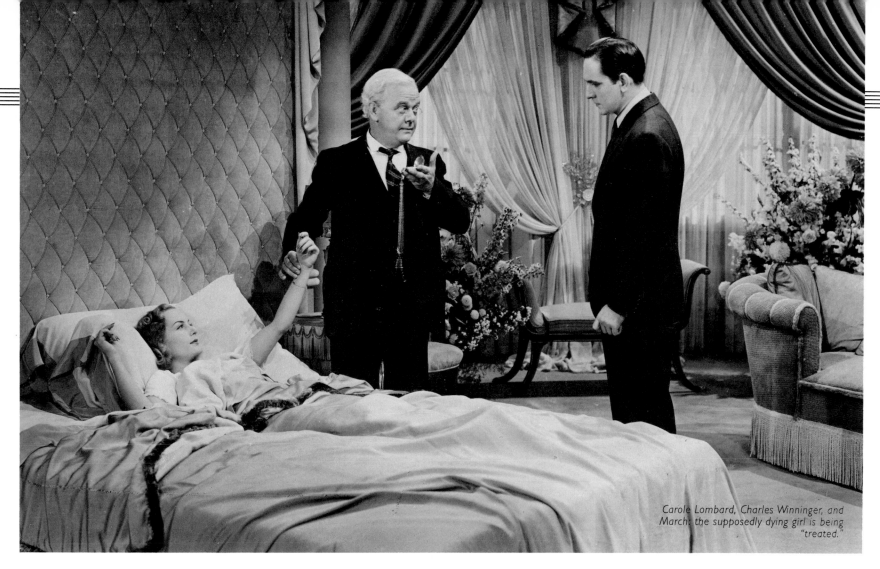

One of the apparent casualties in the growth of realism on the American screen has been the gentlemanly actor, the kind of man who is not only attractive and educated but courtly of manner, well spoken, and thoroughly at home in a dinner jacket. Fredric March had these qualities, and it is a matter of conjecture whether he would be much employed by the contemporary cinema. It would be regrettable if he were not, because March was a fine and versatile actor. Born in Wisconsin in 1897, he decided upon an acting career while a student at the university of that state, even though his family expected him to become a banker. But at the age of twenty his services were required by the United States Army (as an officer, of course), following which he returned to the university to complete his education and receive a degree in economics. He made a living as a bank teller until such time as he could find work in the theatre; he spoke his first lines in a New York play in 1920 and eked out a living over the next few years with bit parts in the theatre, modeling jobs, and work as an extra in movies. By 1925 he was a leading player and four years later made a fairly easy transition to Hollywood because he was exactly what the new talkies needed – a handsome, well-trained actor with a fine speaking voice.

Fredric March, unlike most actors who left New York for Hollywood, never gave up the stage. All through his years of movie stardom he was kept too busy to work in the theatre but once his peak as a movie star had passed – by the early forties – he returned to the stage and achieved remarkable success. From then on he divided his energies between Broadway and Hollywood, and he was one of the few actors to win as much popularity in the one medium as the other.

March had a wide range as a film actor. He was at home in costume, playing historical characters like Mark Twain, Christopher Columbus, Robert Browning, and the Earl of Bothwell, and just as much at ease in modern dress as Norman Maine in *A Star Is Born* and the president of the United States in *Seven Days in May*. In 1931 he won an Oscar for *Dr. Jekyll and Mr. Hyde*, and in

Reporter, heroine, and
editor: the dilemma of a
hoax.

1946 he received another for his banker in *The Best Years of Our Lives*. March sometimes played men who had touches of pomposity about them, even a little greed and lechery, but he seldom did anything to shatter his image as an American gentleman. The nearest he came to being ungentlemanly was his Wally Cook, the ambitious newspaperman of *Nothing Sacred*. David O. Selznick offered him the part while March was completing his role in *A Star Is Born*, and the actor immediately accepted because he welcomed the chance for a little comedy, especially one that would pair him with the divine Carole Lombard. The fact that it would have an original script by Ben Hecht, known for his sometimes stinging wit and his flair for satire, made it an offer hard to decline. Director William Wellman felt the same way and turned from *A Star Is Born* to *Nothing Sacred* without even a break.

Nothing Sacred is as good as its title. By the time its swift seventy-five minutes have passed, Hecht has stuck his needles into the medical profession, small-town respectability,

newspaper ethics, and the ephemeral nature of public sentiment. The story begins in the little Vermont town of Warsaw when Hazel Flagg (Lombard) is told by Dr. Downer (Charles Winninger) that she is suffering from radium poisoning and has only a few months to live. The dithery doctor later finds he has made a big mistake and that Hazel is perfectly healthy, but by this time the news of the rare case has come to the ears of a slick New York City reporter, Wally Cook. He seizes it as an opportunity to write a sensational story and boost the circulation of his paper, which will get him back in the good graces of his perpetually apoplectic editor, Stone (Walter Connolly). Wally is currently demoted to writing obituaries for making the paper look foolish with his yarn about a black New Yorker being an African sultan. Wally sees his chance to write a string of attention getters as he covers the life of a dying young girl.

March K.O.'s Lombard: one of Hollywood's more violent love scenes.

Wally arrives in Warsaw, and after being snarled at by the natives and bitten on the leg by a boy he wonders about the fabled hospitality of small towners. He sells Hazel on the idea of maintaining the story about her demise and points out the good time she can have as he strings people along. Since she hates Warsaw and has been longing to visit New York, she readily agrees. Wally convinces Stone of the publicity value of the story and devises a spectacular campaign. Sympathy and generosity greet her at every turn. The lovely but tragic heroine has the whole country weeping for her. In New York she is wined and dined and feted. A banquet is held in her honor, and an unctuous master of ceremonies (Frank Fay) presides over a lavish tableau, with models representing the celebrated brave ladies of history, such as Helen of Troy, Lady Godiva, Pocahontas, Salome, and Catherine the Great, to all of whom Hazel is compared. She is also given a parade, ending with a presentation by the mayor of the keys to the city. When she visits a nightclub the merrymaking comes to a halt as a mark of respect, and when she and Wally attend a wrestling match the crowd stands to observe a few moments of silence for the stricken girl. Sneers Wally, "For good, clean fun, there's nothing like a wake." Responds fun-loving Hazel, "Oh, please, let's not talk shop." Millions daily read Wally's column, and Hazel becomes America's sweetheart. At a banquet in her honor Hazel has too much to drink and passes out, but Wally merely takes advantage of the situation – he gently picks her up and carries her out, and tears are shed by those who believe her collapse is because of her affliction. But Hazel maintains good health, which finally arouses the suspicions of Stone and the people who have sponsored Hazel's stay in New York.

Stone brings a team of doctors to Hazel's hotel in order to determine her true condition. Wally wants to keep the hoax going and roughs her up to make her look miserable, even clipping her on the chin to send her into unconsciousness. The ruse works for a while longer, but the truth eventually surfaces. Stone, the sponsors, and a group of prominent citizens are now concerned that they will all be made fools when the truth is revealed, and they ask Hazel if she will let it be known that she has died. Hazel obliges them. Now tired of it all, she is also in love with the irrepressible Wally. He proposes, she accepts, and they steal away for a honeymoon in some distant place as the newspaper sadly announces her death and the governor of New York declares a holiday to mark her funeral.

Ben Hecht was himself a veteran newspaperman and he did not spare his fellow members of the fourth estate in this acrid

The lovers preparing their escape.

comedy. His script held up the mirror to the art of ballyhoo and the hypocrisy of vested interests. In 1953 his script was the basis for the Broadway musical *Hazel Flagg*, and a year later Dean Martin and Jerry Lewis used it for their *Living It Up*, with Jerry doing the Hazel part. But neither those versions nor any others that might arise are likely to take the sharp edge off the 1937 original. The combination of Selznick, Wellman, March, and Lombard was unique, and *Nothing Sacred* is one of the reasons why the Golden Age of Hollywood was golden.

Rehearsal scene from Second Chorus.

Fred Astaire no more needs further compliments than does the ceiling of the Sistine Chapel. Suffice to say that there was never anyone like him before he came to Hollywood, never anyone like him during his years of stardom and, as Gene Kelly says, "Fifty years from now, the only one of today's dancers who will be remembered is Fred Astaire." But it is not only as a dancer that Astaire deserves his niche in movie history. He was also a good actor, who carried off his roles pleasingly and convincingly. As a singer he was quite special. The light baritone was not a great instrument, but the diction and the phrasing amounted to genuine style. More great songs were written directly for him than any other performer. Gershwin wrote for him and so did Jerome Kern, Irving Berlin, Cole Porter, Arthur Schwartz, Harry Warren, and Harold Arlen. In short, the involvement of Fred Astaire in the history of American music is spellbinding.

His is also one of the longest careers ever charted. He began his dancing lessons in 1904, when he was five. He and his older sister Adele made a name for themselves as children in their native Omaha, Nebraska, as they appeared in school and church productions, and they were still children when they toured in vaudeville. Their mother functioned as teacher as well as manager. In 1916 the Astaires were hired for their first Broadway production, *Over the Top*, followed by a string of similar engagements until 1922 when a musical was written especially for them – *For Goodness Sake*. By the time Gershwin wrote *Lady Be Good* for them in 1924 they were well established, and with his *Funny Face* three years later Fred and Adele were stars of the first magnitude. After the success of the revue *The Bandwagon* in 1931 Adele left the business and married an English noble, and the nervous Fred was left to find his way as a soloist. Porter's *The Gay Divorcée* in 1932 proved he had nothing to worry about, but the idea of going on with a stage career did not appeal to him, and he asked an agent to try and get him work in Hollywood. Despite his acclaim Astaire was not looked upon as good movie material. Samuel Goldwyn signed him and let him go after a few months, but RKO was in the process of putting together a musical called *Flying Down to Rio* and they needed a pair of dancers for the second leads. They picked Astaire and Ginger Rogers. She and Fred had met while she was a show girl in New York in the early thirties and the idea of appearing together was agreeable to both. The teaming proved to be, to say the least, somewhat successful.

After eight smash hits with Astaire, Ginger Rogers decided to end the teaming and strike out for nonmusical movies, which

Fred Astaire and Paulette Goddard.

The "students" and the secretary.

turned out to be a wise decision for her. It left Astaire, however, in the same spot he had been when his sister left. Over the years he would dance with the best lady dancers Hollywood could offer, particularly Rita Hayworth and Cyd Charisse, but he would never again limit himself to a single partner. Following his split with Rogers he went to MGM to appear with Eleanor Powell in *Broadway Melody of 1940*, but there was never a question of them teaming – she was too much a star in her own right and a soloist at that. Next he went to Paramount and there picked Paulette Goddard to be his co-star in an amusing item titled *Second Chorus*, which was lighter on dancing than his previous pictures and leaned more toward comedy.

In *Second Chorus* Astaire is Danny O'Neill, a college boy well beyond school age, as is Hank Taylor (Burgess Meredith). They are musicians who perpetually and deliberately flunk all their courses in order to stay on at their Ivy League college and operate their profitable dance band. Both are trumpeters and Danny is also the conductor. Both are also inclined to chase the same girls. One night he charms the visiting Ellen Miller (Paulette Goddard) but later finds that the piece of paper on which she has written her phone number is a summons for nonpayment on an encyclopedia given him by Hank. They both like her so much they decide to get her fired by telling her boss she tried to bribe them. The ruse works and Ellen becomes their manager, surprising even herself by doing a good job of booking them. But one day Hank inadvertently correctly answers some test questions and finds himself graduated, and Danny finds himself expelled.

When Artie Shaw and his band play the college, Shaw finds out Ellen is a band manager, hires her himself, and takes her back to New York, which causes Danny and Hank to follow because they both want to win her love. She tries to get them positions with the Shaw band but their practical jokes turn Shaw off. Salvation comes their way in the form of a wealthy patron of the arts, Mr. Chisholm (Charles Butterworth), who is tone deaf but loves music. They convince him of the value of sponsoring an original composition in his honor and of having it performed by Shaw, which is fine by Chisholm provided he can play his mandolin. On the evening of the concert Hank detains Chisholm in his hotel room but accidentally gives himself sleeping pills as well as Chisholm and thereby misses his chance to play trumpet with the Shaw band. Danny wins great approval with his novel dance direction of the band with his "Poor Mr. Chisholm" number, and Ellen afterwards tells him that if he will cut out the jokes and the clowning and settle down to success she will be his girl.

Burgess Meredith and Fred Astaire try to persuade an unimpressed Artie Shaw (center) to use their music.

Astaire dancing with the Shaw orchestra.

Charles Butterworth, Goddard,
Shaw, Meredith, and Astaire.

The material is lightweight, but the assets of Astaire and Shaw in the same picture are considerable. Shaw, one of the more cerebral of bandsmen, appears to advantage in playing his own "Clarinet Concerto," a short and effective piece for solo clarinet and swing band, and he also wrote the film's attractive main song, "Love of My Life," with lyrics by Johnny Mercer. The song is stylishly sung by Astaire to Goddard and later reprised in a Russian restaurant scene as Astaire does it with a heavy Russian accent, followed by a native dance, the *prisiadka*. Since neither Astaire nor Meredith could play trumpet for their roles, they were dubbed, respectively, by the superb Bobby Hackett and Billy Butterfield, both of whom are also visible as members of Shaw's fine band.

Paulette Goddard acquitted herself well in her principal dance routine, "I Ain't Hep to That Step but I'll Dig It," a largely jive number in which the lyrics emerge from conversation in the form of rhyming couplets. Astaire also does a solo with "The New Moon Is Rising," but his grandest efforts are reserved for the finale, when he conducts the Shaw band and dances at the same time, a sequence that was filmed at the Wilshire Ebell Theatre in Los Angeles. What most attracted Astaire to *Second Chorus* was the chance to be involved with Artie Shaw and the other jazz musicians. Astaire is a good jazz pianist, and he is also a song writer. He has recorded four of his songs: "Not My Girl," "If Swing Goes, I Go Too," "City of the Angels," and "Life Is Wonderful," but he admits they haven't brought him as much acclaim as he had wished. He is willing to settle for his success as a dancer. It is, of course, quite something for which to settle.

Astaire dance-conducting the Shaw orchestra.

75

Dead drunk and
fallen downstairs:
Kirk Douglas's
screen debut.

Lizabeth Scott and Van Heflin arrive in town at the opening of The Strange Love of Martha Ivers.

FOUR

DARK SHADES ON THE AMERICAN SCENE

The general image of Kirk Douglas as a tough, forceful, tenacious man was not apparent in his first film. In *The Strange Love of Martha Ivers* Douglas appeared as a weak, alcoholic, spiritually bankrupt man, dominated by a vicious wife and made a criminal by her. It was an effective performance, and it began a long and still potent career in Hollywood. The assertive Douglas image is very much an extension of the man and very much an American image. Douglas is, in fact, one of the film industry's most perfect examples of the Horatio Alger story. His parents were illiterate Russian immigrants who settled in Amsterdam, New York, in 1910, where their son Issur Danielovitch was born in December of 1916. He was the only son in a family of six daughters, all of whom had to work while still children in order to keep the family above the poverty line. Douglas claims to have had more than forty jobs, mostly menial, prior to becoming an actor, an ambition he set for himself while in high school. At seventeen, having managed to save $163, he hitchhiked to Canton, New York, and prevailed upon the dean of St. Lawrence University to award him a scholarship. The dean decided to give the very determined young man a chance

and arranged a small loan and part-time jobs as gardener, waiter, and janitor. By the end of his four years Douglas had excelled as both a debater and a wrestler, and had become president of the student body and the college dramatic group. He was clearly a young man who would do well in life, since he not only had talent and personality but the driving force of a battering ram. That, too, is in line with the American image and the way Americans like to see themselves – as people who seize opportunity and ram their way through the difficulties.

Once graduated from college, Kirk Douglas's next objective was the American Academy of Dramatic Art in New York. The administrators explained to him that no scholarships were

available, but the fledgling actor thereupon did an audition for them that was so persuasive they made an exception. He lived in a settlement house in Greenwich Village, working at odd jobs to support himself and earning his first income as an actor during the summer with stock companies. It was at this time he decided to change his name, picking Douglas because of his admiration for Douglas Fairbanks, Sr., and Kirk simply because it appealed to him. His first professional job came when Guthrie McClintic hired him for a bit part as a singing telegram boy in *Spring Again*, but his attempts to expand his career were then interrupted by a call to the colors in early 1942. Douglas joined the navy and served as an ensign with an antisubmarine unit in the Pacific. He was injured in action and given a medical discharge in late 1944, after which he returned to New York.

Douglas's first break came when he was able to take over Richard Widmark's role in *Kiss and Tell*. Parts in other plays and some work in radio followed. It was Lauren Bacall, who had been a classmate at the American Academy, who brought Douglas to Hollywood's attention. She persuaded Hal B. Wallis to take a look at Douglas on his next trip to New York. Wallis was impressed with Douglas and offered him a test but the actor was doing well in the play *The Wind Is Ninety* and declined. Later, with the play closed and no follow-up job, he went to the Paramount

office in New York and asked to be put in touch with Wallis. Wallis was as good as his word. He tested Douglas, liked him, and gave him fourth billing in *The Strange Love of Martha Ivers*. At the age of thirty, Kirk Douglas made a fairly quick and easy entry into movie fame.

The Strange Love of Martha Ivers is a black jigsaw of a story, full of ruthless, nasty people engaged in extortion and murder. It is an unlikely melodrama, but it is made fascinating by the elements used by the shrewd Wallis, notably the script of Robert Rossen, the darkly-hued score by Miklos Rozsa, and the firm direction of Lewis Milestone, who was a master of realism. His was a fluid camera style, impersonal rather than personal, which was perfect for this film since it gave a chilling, matter-of-fact atmosphere to an improbable set of characters and circumstances.

The film deals with one of those family towns so popular in American fiction, towns ruled over by a powerful and often unjust family, who transcend free enterprise and become almost fascistic. Here the town is Iverstown, Pennsylvania, and the ruler is Martha Ivers (Barbara Stanwyck), who has allowed an innocent man to go to the gallows to cover up her own accidental slaying of her aunt (Judith Anderson). The aunt was a dictator, both in running the factory which dominates the town, and with

Heflin connives with
Stanwyck to rid her of her
husband.

Heflin and Douglas: the
death struggle.

80

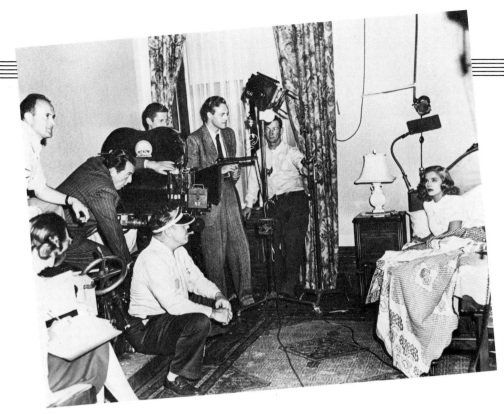

On the set with director Lewis Milestone in the pin-stripe suit.

her family. One of her employees, O'Neil (Roman Bohnen), has insinuated himself into her confidence. He witnesses thirteen-year-old Martha killing her aunt, in an attempt to save her cat from being hit by the aunt. O'Neil then assumes command over the girl by backing up her story that the slaying was done by a stranger. Martha as a woman runs Iverstown in much the same manner as her aunt and marries O'Neil's son Walter (Kirk Douglas) as part of the price of his silence. It is a cold and empty marriage, and Martha despises Walter, who has, because of her power, assumed the office of district attorney.

Seventeen years after the slaying, Sam Masterson (Van Heflin) returns to Iverstown and causes consternation because both Martha and Walter believe that Sam was a witness to the death of the aunt. Sam was a boyfriend, but he did not actually see the killing and left town shortly thereafter. He returns with the reputation of a gambler, which worries Walter who assumes Sam is out for blackmail. Martha, who openly carries on love affairs as Walter drowns his sorrows in drink, is attracted to Sam. He responds to her when he senses there is something strange about her references to her aunt and about their friendship as youngsters, and the truth finally dawns upon him. In the meantime, Walter, in an attempt to scare Sam out of town, has Sam's girlfriend, Toni (Lizabeth Scott), beaten up. This serves only to make Sam more determined to learn all the facts in the mystery. He examines newspaper accounts and concludes that an innocent man was sent to the gallows on perjured evidence.

With a clear picture of what happened and how the Ivers have run the town, Sam visits Martha and Walter, with the idea of profiting on his knowledge.

Walter, well into his cups, admits their corruption and their love for riches and power. When he falls drunkenly downstairs, Martha urges Sam to kill him. He turns on her, saying, "You're sick, you don't even know what's right and wrong." Martha justifies herself, claiming that those who were killed and ruined by the Ivers were people of no account and besides, "Look what I've done with what she left me – I've given to charity, built schools, hospitals. I've given thousands of people work." At this revelation of moral decay Sam decides to forget his plans for extortion and simply leave Iverstown forever and take Toni with him. As he leaves the house Martha, gun in hand, asks Walter to help her kill Sam. To her surprise and fear, Walter, for the first time in his life, turns on her and expresses his contempt and bitterness. But he rationalizes, "It's not anybody's fault, it's just the way things are. It's what people want and how hard they want it, and how hard it is for them to get it." Realizing that it cannot go on and that their sins have trapped them, Walter shoots Martha and then kills himself.

The Strange Love of Martha Ivers is an evil tale, but like so many other stories of wicked people involved in dreadful doings, it casts a certain spell. It is a minor masterpiece of film noir, expertly manufactured by craftsmen and deftly played by the indelible likes of Barbara Stanwyck, Van Heflin, and Kirk Douglas.

David O. Selznick created the world's most perfect popular movie in *Gone With the Wind* and then spent the rest of his life unsuccessfully trying to do better. Orson Welles gave himself a similar problem by making *Citizen Kane* in his first attempt at film making, and created one of the world's truly classic movies. He was a mere twenty-five years of age at the time, and although he has made other interesting pictures, both as director and actor, it is doubtful if he will ever again make a *Kane*. Perhaps he can take comfort in knowing that no other American film maker has made one either.

Welles was sixteen when he visited Dublin during a vacation in 1931. A midwesterner by birth and education, he had first considered a career as an artist and went to Ireland to do sketches. But he took a notion to visit the famed Abbey Gate Theatre in Dublin and convinced them that he was an actor, which they instantly believed and hired him. Back in America three years later he organized and managed the Woodstock, Illinois, Theatre Festival and thereafter became a "boy wonder" of the American theatrical world by directing and acting in a number of plays. In 1937, age twenty-two, he was made a director of the Federal Theatre Project in New York and later

the same year, with John Houseman, founded his successful Mercury Theatre, beginning with the modern-day version of *Julius Caesar* that brought his company much attention. Their radio productions, particularly *The War of the Worlds*, brought them even more.

Nothing about Orson Welles's early years was ordinary or usual. While other would-be film producers found Hollywood a bastion that could be broken into only with tremendous effort and time, Welles was invited by RKO to make a film for them – a film of his own choice. With a budget of $750,000 and his own players he chose to attack the power of the press and the corruption caused by ambition and greed. Unfortunately *Citizen*

Loretta Young, the wife who begins to fear that her husband (Orson Welles) was a Nazi: The Stranger.

One Nazi finds another:
Konstantin Shayne and
Welles.

Welles playing checkers
with Billy House.

The wife's apprehension grows deeper.

Kane resembled the life and style of William Randolph Hearst, whose power was at that time colossal. Consequently *Kane* did very poor business at the box office. In time it has become not only an item of study but one of the more trenchant film attacks on the outer extremes of the American scene.

A year later Welles tackled another slice of Americana, Booth Tarkington's *The Magnificent Ambersons*, the story of a turn-of-the century rich American family unwilling to change with the times. Taken out of his hands for the editing, it failed with the public, again partly due to Hearst clout, but like *Kane* it too is an item for film study. After that Welles had to settle for offers as an actor, which always brought attention and acclaim, especially his Mr. Rochester in *Jane Eyre* (1944). He

Her father (Philip Merivale) and a federal investigator (Edward G. Robinson) warn her of her husband's true identity.

took a small role in the Eric Ambler espionage yarn *Journey into Fear* and helped produce it, but it wasn't until 1946 that he was given another chance to direct a film. Producer Sam Spiegel admired *Citizen Kane* and wanted to work with him. He offered him the lead in *The Stranger* and Welles accepted – provided he could also direct.

In making his understanding with Welles, Spiegel laid down his ground rules. Welles would have to stick to the script as written, he would have to keep to the shooting schedule, and he would have to follow the editing requirements as supervised by Spiegel. Welles agreed to these terms – and followed them. *The Stranger* was filmed in thirty-five days, under schedule, under

budget, and with no untoward incidents during the making. The "boy wonder" proved to be no problem at all, and Spiegel was well pleased with the results, which turned out to be an intelligent thriller and one of the first Hollywood pictures to deal with the postwar attempts to track down Nazi criminals.

The title character is a cultured German professor, Charles Rankin (Welles), who has been hired by the Harper School for Boys in a small Connecticut town. In Germany a minor Nazi criminal, Meinike (Konstantin Shayne), is allowed to escape in order that he will seek out his infamous superior, Franz Kindler, who has made his way to South America and possibly to the United States. A war crimes official, Wilson (Edward G. Robin-

The wife's life at stake.

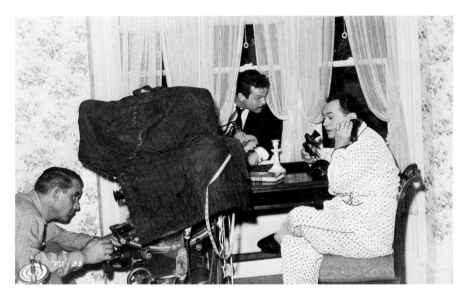

Welles, as director, sets up one of his famous low-angle shots.

son), tracks Meinike, and the trail leads to the town in Connecticut. Wilson catches up with Meinike in the Harper school, but the ex-Nazi becomes aware of Wilson and knocks him out. In trying to reach Rankin, who is Kindler, Meinike meets Mary Longstreet (Loretta Young), who is about to marry Rankin. The professor makes an appointment to meet Meinike in the nearby woods and there learns that all their former colleagues have been captured. Meinike, now a religious fanatic, begs Rankin to renounce his past and pray to God, but Rankin knows why Meinike has been allowed to escape, and he kills and buries him on the spot.

Rankin comforts himself that he has married the daughter of an American supreme court judge and is therefore hardly likely to be detected. Wilson is suspicious when he talks to Rankin and picks up clues about his political leanings. Posing as an art collector, Wilson finds out that Rankin is an authority on clocks and that he is fascinated by the town's clock, which is a genuine Strasbourg Hobrecht. In talking to Mary he tells her about Franz Kindler, "one of the most brilliant of the younger minds in the Nazi Party" and the architect of its genocide program. Kindler, he tells her, was an expert on clocks. He shows her films of Nazi atrocities, but she recoils from the implication that her husband is Kindler. Her father, however, is convinced by Wilson, who warns him that Mary's life is in danger.

Rankin attends to his new hobby, the restoration of the Strasbourg clock in the tower, more than a hundred feet above the town square. He saws through a rung of the ladder and later arranges for his wife to visit him in the tower, hoping she will thereby fall to her death and not reveal her doubts about his identity. She is saved by Wilson and her father, but she later resolves to climb to the top of the tower and kill her husband. He proudly proclaims his innocence: "I only followed orders. I only did my duty. I am not a criminal." Kindler/Rankin now meets his death. With obvious symbolic irony he is impaled on the figure of the Avenging Angel in the revolving clock tower.

The Stranger is given its distinction by Orson Welles, by his presence as the cultured, quietly arrogant Nazi and by his direction. The film is neat and precise, as if reflecting the brilliant organizational mind of its title character. And the horror represented by that character is a dramatically startling contrast to the peaceful, benign little American town in which he takes refuge. American values are also pointed up by the script's reference to Ralph Waldo Emerson: "Commit a crime and the earth is made of glass." Wilson, the war-crimes detective, further quotes Emerson on the subject of crime: "You cannot draw up the ladder so as to leave no inlet or clue," which the finale of *The Stranger* graphically proves as the villain plunges to his death. The theory that the evil and the greedy build their own destruction is as apparent in this film as in the two first classics by Welles. In this and in other films Orson Welles has jolted the complacency of American innocence and reminded Americans that they are not entirely removed from the forces that have corrupted other civilizations. A Nazi, it seems, can even be found in postcard-picturesque Connecticut.

Garfield as the prize fighter on the way down in They Made Me a Criminal.

FIVE

IT'S A CRIME

John Garfield: the beginning of a new, more earthy American image.

Crime is a vital part of the picture business. Just how much actual crime takes place behind the Hollywood scenes is open to conjecture, but crime enacted before the cameras is a veritable gusher of profit. Murder, robbery, corruption, arson, adultery, piracy, and graft – where would the business of movie making be without them? Or actors who can convincingly play the hoodlums and crooks? Ironically some of the actors who have excelled in these roles have been men who in their real lives would scarcely hurt a fly. John Garfield was not a happy man away from the cameras, but he was never known to be violent or unmannerly. Edward G. Robinson, the personification of *Little Caesar*, was about as gentle as a man could be. The fact that Paul Muni could terrify audiences as *Scarface* is astonishing in view of his mild, passive nature. James Cagney for far too long persuaded moviegoers that he was a pugnacious delinquent, but as anyone who knows Cagney can testify, he is a quiet, dreamy sort of man, who writes poetry and studies modern methods of farming. They were all, of course, superb film actors and the playing of gangsters was only part of their success, albeit an indelible part.

The boxer and the good-time gal, Ann Sheridan.

Audiences in 1938 went to see Warners' *Four Daughters* expecting it to be a sentimental, glossy family picture. They found it to be that and more. The "more" was a twenty-five-year-old actor named John Garfield, who played a rough-mannered drifter with a chip on his shoulder about the way the world has treated him. He is a sardonic misfit from the other side of the tracks but a young man of ability and vitality, and of the opinion he deserves better. The public immediately took to Garfield. He was different. He wasn't tall and handsome but he was real – more real than the usual movie male. Hollywood had always projected a fantasized view of American family life, especially the middle-class, small-town version, but suddenly Garfield appeared in the fanciful *Four Daughters* and the picture stopped being fanciful. The "outsider" was now "in."

Garfield was born Julius Garfinkle in New York City in May of 1913. He was a product of the harsh life of the impoverished, and his values were those he picked up in surviving on the streets. His salvation was a Bronx school teacher, Angelo Patri, who realized the boy's abilities and encouraged him to study speech in order to overcome a stutter and to partake of school plays to give him confidence. His life started to change. When he was fourteen Julius won the *New York Times* city-wide oratorical contest, speaking on the subject of Benjamin Franklin. Patri then arranged for him to be given a scholarship to the Heckscher

A Dead End Kid finds his idol.

Foundation, a school where he learned about acting and where he resolved to make it his career.

He was seventeen when he started out to make his living, and he could hardly have picked a worse time – the first years of the Depression. But he was determined, and he accepted anything that any theatre could give him, from sweeping up to carrying a spear in costume plays. He was taken on as an apprentice by Eva Le Gallienne for her Civic Repertory Company and carried more spears, but he also had the chance to learn from top professionals. In 1932 he was offered a part in the touring company of *Counselor-at-Law* and from that engagement gradually came bits in other companies. Julius became friendly with a young Bronx writer named Clifford Odets, who had joined a group of young actors to set up their own group, with the support of the Theatre Guild. They called themselves the Group Theatre, and by 1935 they were an avant-garde presence in the New York theatrical community. Some of the others in the group were Elia Kazan, Luther Adler, Franchot Tone, and Lee Strasberg. Julius was eager and willing, and his ambition was sparked by contact with people of this calibre. When the group performed a play Odets had written for them, *Awake and Sing*, Jules Garfield, as he was now called, was given a leading role. There were roles in other plays, and in 1937 Garfield made a strong impression in Odets's *Golden Boy*.

91

had assumed that he would return to the stage after making the film, but he had been unaware of the power of movie success. Warners signed him to a seven-year contract, and like every actor they had under contract he would go from film to film. For his second picture he was given the lead and promoted as a star. They pulled out the script of their 1933 movie *The Life of Jimmy Dolan*, which had starred Douglas Fairbanks, Jr., as a boxer who accidentally kills a man but redeems himself in the eyes of society by helping invalid children, and gave it to Sig Herzig to reshape for Garfield. The title *They Made Me a Criminal* clearly indicated the image they wanted for their new personality – a bit of Bogart, a touch of Cagney, and a strong emphasis on the odd-man-out, going against the grain of society. Garfield would increasingly represent the American ethnic elements, the not-so-pretty people who have to try harder, but it was an image that did not fully do justice to his talent as an actor. He had broken the type-cast mold of the conventional movie leading man but then became trapped in the image with which he did it.

The title *They Made Me a Criminal* is misleading because the protagonist, Johnny Burns, does not actually resort to crime. He becomes a fugitive and tries to elude the police, but it comes about as the result of an accident. Johnny is a successful boxer with his own style, but his social life is far from admirable, as he cavorts with underworld people. At a party in which he has too much to drink, a man is killed in a fight, and Johnny assumes that he must be the culprit. At least, that's what his so-called friends want him to believe. They advise him to get as far away from New York as he can. He drifts across America and ends up hitch-hiking in California, and in need of work. He drops off at a fruit ranch and begs for something to eat in return for a little work. The kindly old lady (May Robson) who runs the place takes a liking to him and gives him a job.

The job brings him into conflict with the six New York roughnecks (the Dead End Kids) being rehabilitated by the owner, who look upon him as a hobo on the make for the owner's pretty daughter, Peggy (Gloria Dickson), until he teaches them how to box. Then he becomes their hero. But the real test of his character comes when his benefactors are faced with eviction because of lack of funds. Johnny returns to the ring to fight a barnstorming pugilist, even though he knows he risks being recognized. Detective Phelan (Claude Rains), who has been trailing Johnny ever since his flight from New York, sees the fight and moves to arrest Johnny. But the charge is not one of murder, which has been solved. Phelan now has to bring in Johnny on a charge of leaving the scene of a crime and evading

The Group Theatre had not escaped the notice of Hollywood talent scouts, and during the run of *Golden Boy* Garfield was offered a part in a movie. It meant leaving the play, which annoyed the other members of the group, but Garfield was now a married man with a child and needed more than the small income of an insecure stage actor. After playing his part in *Four Daughters* Garfield expected to return to New York, but the film's director, Michael Curtiz, sensed Garfield's film potential so strongly that he altered the dramatic focus of the movie and played up Garfield. The actor always allowed that his screen persona had much to do with this director. "I would normally have been a character actor, but Mike Curtiz gave me the screen personality that carried me to stardom."

Garfield – with the Jules now changed to John by Warners –

Fritz Lang's success in Hollywood points to a very American fact of life – the peculiar force of the melting pot. American culture is an amalgam of many styles from many sources, and this is more true of the movies than of any other form of American entertainment. Much of the talent came from elsewhere, but under the able leadership of the moguls it blended into a style and a direction that had great relevance for Americans. In fact, the American cinema would not have risen to its heights and its potential without this influx of directors, writers, actors, composers, and photographers from abroad, especially from England and Germany. They not only contributed their considerable abilities, but they spotted the characteristics and drifts of American life perhaps more perceptively than the natives. The eyes, ears, and mind of a man like Fritz Lang had much to do with telling Americans things about themselves.

Scarlet Street may be regarded as typical of Lang's ability to comment on the human failings that can turn life into a nightmare. The year previous he had made the well received *Woman in the Window*, with Edward G. Robinson as a cultured professor who falls in love with a young woman (Joan Bennett) and comes to grief when he accidentally kills her lover and is afterwards plagued by a blackmailer (Dan Duryea). The fault with that otherwise excellent *film noir* is the ending, when the professor awakens and realizes it has all been a dream. But the teaming of Lang, Robinson, Bennett, and Duryea was so striking that the critics and the public were ready for another picture from them, albeit one with a more satisfying ending.

In *Scarlet Street* Robinson is a drab, middle-aged man named Christopher Cross, who works as a cashier in a clothing store and paints canvases as a hobby and as a means of escaping his bitter shrew of a wife (Rosalind Ivan), whose tyranny is so great that the poor man has to retreat to the bathroom and do his painting while sitting on the edge of the tub. His romantic fantasies find expression in his paintings, while his wife scoffs at him and never lets him forget that she was once his landlady and that by marrying her he received board and lodgings. At a banquet honoring his twenty years of service as the company's cashier, Cross is awarded a gold watch and praised for his fidelity and honesty. Cross has a little too much champagne, and while walking home he comes across a man beating a young woman, and he goes to her defense, warding off the man with his umbrella. He takes the girl, Kitty March (Bennett), to a nearby bar and comforts her, and in the course of thanking him she asks him about himself. Too proud to admit to being a cashier, he tells her that he is a painter, from which she assumes that he is

Bennett at the height of her glory in a portrait still from Scarlet Street.

Rosalind Ivan and Edward G. Robinson, the shrewish wife and hen-pecked husband.

successful and well paid. Kitty is a call girl, but she does not let Cross know this, nor that her assailant was her boy friend Johnny (Duryea). Cross becomes infatuated with her, and she leads him on. She persuades Cross to rent an apartment for her and spend as much time as possible with her as her lover, as well as do his paintings in comfort. The idea is agreeable to Cross but within a short while he finds his earnings are not enough to maintain the apartment and Kitty's tastes in clothes.

Kitty is in league with Johnny to take advantage of Cross. Johnny has Cross's paintings appraised and finds that they are considered of merit and of value. He has Kitty sign her name to them and together they make money selling the paintings. Cross eventually finds out, but his love for Kitty and his vanity overcome his anger. He is delighted that his work is praised and he allows her to go on signing her name, but without knowing of the income. Money becomes more and more of a problem for him, and he resorts to stealing from his wife and from his employers. When found out he is fired.

After losing his job Cross returns to the apartment and arrives in time to find Kitty in Johnny's embrace and happily summing up their good fortune. Cross waits for Johnny to leave and then faces Kitty. She taunts him for being a drab little man for whom she cares nothing, and Cross goes berserk with anger. He picks up an icepick and stabs her through the bedclothes. Too timid to call the police, he just slips away into the night. Johnny, who has a police record, is picked up and jailed. The circumstantial evidence points to him as the killer, and he meets his death in the electric chair. Cross takes some pleasure in at first knowing this, but with time it becomes a moral burden and his guilt turns him into a derelict. In delirium he hears Johnny say, "You killed me, Chris. You're old and you're ugly and you killed me." He is also haunted by the mocking voice of Kitty. One evening, dirty and disheveled, he shuffles by the window of an art gallery and sees his portrait, assumed to be a self-portrait, of Kitty. As he looks it is taken from the window and sold for ten thousand dollars – the ultimate comment on a miserably failed life.

Fritz Lang always claimed that his point of view in dealing with these dark studies of human nature and criminality was that the average human is never far removed from the actual criminal and that circumstances can turn ordinary people into monsters. Perhaps it is the truth in that view that makes his films so compelling, especially *Scarlet Street*, in which the lack of courage in Christopher Cross and the weaknesses in his nature cause his decline. It was a study that had long fascinated Lang. Indeed, *Scarlet Street* is his remake of the 1931 French film *La Chienne*

The heartless beauty and her artist slave.

The cheated artist: Robinson spots his paintings for sale.

(The Bitch), directed by Jean Renoir, with the murky Montmartre setting transferred to Manhattan. Lang always worked closely with his photographers, and in this case he had the services of the brilliant Milton Krasner, who also did *Woman in the Window*, and the two men were in accord in the use of dramatic angles, dark lighting, and shadows.

Lang also had the benefit of a score by the Austrian-born composer Hans J. Salter, who like Lang had cut his professional teeth in German film and had left because of the Nazis. Salter joined Universal in 1938 and made a specialty of scoring horror films, and was therefore a natural choice when Lang came to the studio to make *Scarlet Street*. Says Salter: "My recollections of Fritz Lang are only pleasant ones. Although he had a reputation for being difficult and hard to please, we 'hit it off' right from the start and became good friends. Fritz had a pretty clear perception of the role music was going to play in his picture – and so did I. We had some lively discussions before I got started; he made some very constructive suggestions and he liked my ideas, especially the 'shock treatment' of arrested, sustained chords whenever the scene suggested it. After the recording session Fritz was very complimentary of the score – with one exception. The end title bothered him. He said it left too much hope for the character played by Robinson and since the whole idea of his film was 'crime does not pay' there should be a relentless downbeat feeling that implies that the character has to live with his guilt and suffer until the end of his life. I agreed and rewrote it."

The end of the line.

Paul Muni as the judge in Angel on My Shoulder.

If ability were commensurate with popularity in the movies, then Paul Muni would have been a bigger draw than Clark Gable. Muni enjoyed success, but he never sacrificed the art of acting in order to get it. He was not concerned with personality, only with playing a character as best he could, and his reputation for being a slow study and taking great pains to arrive at the end product has few equals in Hollywood annals. On the other hand it was the respect for his ability that won him more time and patience than were afforded most actors in films. The studios in the Golden Age were not much concerned with artistic prestige, but in Muni's case they made an exception. They were savvy enough to know that a little prestige now and then was good for the American image. A little, not too much. Culture wasn't box office.

He was born Muni Weissenfreund in Poland in 1895 and brought to America when he was seven. His parents were itinerant performers who could play everything from vaudeville to serious drama, and managed to make a similar living in their new country. By 1907 they became a part of the Yiddish Theatre in Cleveland, with all of their three sons playing in the theatre band. Muni was encouraged to become a violinist but opted for acting and made his first appearance on stage when he was twelve. By the time he was fifteen he was a professional and a member of a Yiddish touring company; in 1918 he was hired by the esteemed Yiddish Art Theatre in New York.

He was with that company for seven years and received an enviable education, one which led to opportunities in top Broadway productions. In 1929 Fox production chief Winfield Sheehan brought him to Hollywood, changed his name to Paul Muni, and gave him the lead in *The Valiant*, followed by *Seven Faces*. But Muni was not happy with the material offered to him and asked for his release in order to return to the stage. Two years later Howard Hughes asked him to test for the part of Scarface, a role based upon the career of gangster Al Capone. The tough, realistic exposé of crime shot Muni to film fame. In 1932 he was signed by Warner Bros. to a seven-year contract, starting off with the box office winner *I Was a Fugitive from a Chain Gang*. He made only ten films during those seven years, a fraction of the number made by other stars during the same period, but some of those films are classics, particularly the biographical accounts of Louis Pasteur, Emile Zola, and Benito Juarez.

Muni never played himself. Indeed, his appearance changed greatly with every film, although he seldom indulged in the art of make-up. On that subject he said: "Some screen actors who have worked up a tremendous reputation as character men by appearing in different make-up in each picture have never rung true to me because I can see their personality behind their disguises. Their foundation isn't right. In order to characterize effectively it is more important to masquerade the mind than the body. It is possible for a great actor to create the illusion of age, or nationality, or station in life, without once resorting to a beard,

false teeth, or whatever. External devices should be used merely to help an audience believe the role, not to help an actor play it."

After he left Warners in 1939 Muni was economical about his film appearances. He preferred the stage and came back to Hollywood only now and then. In 1946 he accepted Charles Rogers's offer to play in *Angel on My Shoulder* because it allowed him to be a tough gangster again, à la Scarface, but also to balance it with the dual role of a humane judge and to reveal the more human traits in the gangster. The veteran director Archie Mayo was assigned to the film, and there was a degree of friction in the filming because Mayo was used to working very fast and Muni worked only very slowly. He was the kind of actor who liked to probe the meaning of every line.

Muni as the hood in Hell with his guide, Claude Rains.

Muni the hood in the body of the judge with Rains and with the bride-to-be, Anne Baxter.

Angel on My Shoulder was a remake, with changes, of *Here Comes Mr. Jordan* (1941), in which Robert Montgomery starred as a prizefighter who is sent to Heaven before his time and has to find a new body to occupy on his return to Earth. In 1978 Warren Beatty picked up Harry Segall's story again and turned it into the greatly successful *Heaven Can Wait*, altering the lead to that of a football star. But in the 1946 picture the protagonist is a tough, unmannerly gangster named Eddie Kagle.

The film begins with Eddie being released from prison and met by one of his former lieutenants, Smiley (Hardie Albright), who welcomes him back and then kills him. Later Eddie finds himself walking in some strange, fiery, cavernous region, which he soon learns is Hell. To him it is another form of prison from which he is eager to escape, particularly to get even with Smiley. The Devil (Claude Rains) is a cultured, business-like gentleman, who is willing to make a deal with Eddie. It happens that Eddie is the exact double of Judge Frederick Parker, a man who has caused criminals to redeem themselves and avoid ending up in Hell. This offends the Devil, who prefers to have Eddie call him Nick. Nick leads him back to life and the big city, and to the courtroom of Judge Parker, whom they witness collapsing from heart strain and overwork. As the judge lies sleeping in his chamber, Nick hypnotizes Eddie's spirit and merges it with the body of the judge.

Eddie is happy to find himself again with a body and alive, and he resolves to find and kill Smiley. Nick reminds him that he is in his employ and that his job now is to ruin Judge Parker's reputation. The judge's fiancée, Barbara (Anne Baxter), is puzzled and alarmed by his sudden change of manner, his crudeness, and she assumes he must have had some kind of mental breakdown. Since the judge is running for governor, this is very upsetting, especially when he keeps talking to Nick, whom Barbara can't see. Called upon to address a political rally, Eddie becomes a hero when he jumps down from the stage and thrashes a gang of hecklers, which displeases Nick, who was hoping Eddie would make a fool of the judge's image.

Pleased with the new virility shown by the judge, Barbara encourages him all the more to run for governor. One of the hired hecklers points out to the opposition that the judge is the spitting image of the deceased Eddie and that he fights just like him, so there must be a connection. At the trial of a powerful gangster named Bentley the opposition arranges for a large bribe, but Eddie rejects it when he recognizes Bentley's wife (Marion Martin) as one of his former double-crossing cohorts. He loudly declares he cannot be bribed even for a million dollars.

Baxter is curious at the new-found behavior of the judge.

The judge and his fiancée plan their new life.

This brings Judge Parker even more admiration – to the disgust of Nick. But the Devil sees his chance to tarnish Parker when he is able to tell Eddie where he can find Smiley. In the meantime Eddie has fallen in love with Barbara and asks to get married as soon as possible. In being interviewed by the minister who will perform the wedding, Eddie learns that no man can be controlled by the Devil if he listens to the angel on his shoulder and resolves to do only good.

Eddie changes his mind about killing Smiley, but when Smiley sees the man he killed he panics and falls to his death through the window of a high-storied apartment. Nick thereby loses a major point in his control over Eddie. Now realizing how bad his life has been and how good it might have been, Eddie persuades Barbara to delay the wedding a little. He prefers to return to Hell and let Judge Parker have his body, and his life, back. Barbara will then find the happiness she deserves.

The tables are now turned. Nick cannot return to Hell without bringing back Eddie, since it cannot be known that he was a failure in his latest earthly foray. Eddie agrees to keep it all a secret provided Nick will let the judge alone. Nick declares he will put Eddie through the rages of his domain, but Eddie demands to be made a trusty in return for his silence. Nick knows he has no choice.

Apart from the pleasure of watching Paul Muni doing a slightly comedic version of his famed *Scarface* persona, *Angel on My Shoulder* is of further interest because of the presence of Claude Rains. He had played the emissary from Heaven in *Here Comes Mr. Jordan*, but whether from that region or from Hades he was deftly amusing. Rains had an impish quality and a dry, cultivated English diction that made his acting arresting as well as effective. His sly by-play with Muni in *Angel on My Shouder* is a major reason for taking another look at this satiric American morality play. The term "morality play" was not one the moguls would have condoned in that Golden Age. Suffice for them to call it a comedy. But *Angel on My Shoulder* is definitely an American kind of satire, one which pricks the balloons of civic-political conniving and the attempts of the underworld to infiltrate the judicial system. The law is a more massive industry in America than in any other country, and many miles of film have played with that fact, sometimes dramatically but mostly satirically. American satire often has a very sharp sting. The contrasting images of Paul Muni as hoodlum and judge is a good example.

Blood on the Sun: *James Cagney, the tough American newspaperman on assignment in Japan...*
... and Sylvia Sidney, the beautiful, mysterious Eurasian.

In reviewing *Blood on the Sun*, the distinguished British critic C.A. Lejeune noted: "James Cagney is one of the best screen actors of our time, with gifts of pathos and an impish humor second to none.... With no hint of a four-dimensional character to work from, little material to suggest the hero's past and background, or even his tastes and way of living, Mr. Cagney is content to convey all the immediate reactions of a man who is exuberantly alive today and expects to be terribly dead tomorrow. It is a lesson to all young film actors to study how he does this.... Few heroes of melodrama can claim that so much skill of such high order has been spent in bringing their poor bones to life."

In 1980, after twenty years of retirement, James Cagney was persuaded to return to the screen to play a cameo role in *Ragtime*. To his friends and admirers it was as much a surprise as a delight. When Cagney finished his work in Billy Wilder's *One Two Three* in 1960 he declared his film career over and complete. He had enjoyed thirty years in the movies, but now it was at an end – and anyone who knew Cagney knew that when he said something, he meant it. He flatly refused all offers to return to the screen, until his doctor advised him that it would be good for

Wallace Ford, Cagney's dead friend, and the Japanese officials who killed him.

James Bell and Cagney, newspapermen on the trail of espionage.

his health to do a little of the work that had made him a legend in film history. So, at the age of eighty, Cagney took the doctor's advice and thereby added a footnote to a vivid and vital career.

The Cagney image is assertive and alert and buoyantly alive. In dozens of films of the thirties the image was that of a pugnacious young man battling the elements of a hostile world and surviving, except on those occasions when he was a criminal and paid society's price. But even as a gangster Cagney was an arresting figure, ever quick and dynamic and aware of all the shadings of human nature. It was an image culled from his own working-class background in New York City, but it was largely a false image. In person Cagney was never tough or abrasive. Acting was business and the image was his *modus operandi*. Despite a lack of formal education Cagney became a cultured man, with a large library and extended interests in certain subjects, such as the American Civil War and soil conservation. His lifestyle has never been Hollywoodish; married to the same lady for almost sixty years, Cagney could hardly have been more circumspect had he been a minister.

Born on the lower East Side of Manhattan in July of 1899, Cagney's bloodlines are mostly Irish, with a dash of Norwegian, and he knew what it was like to work hard for a living at an early age. He held after-school jobs to help with the family income. After graduating from high school he took a fine arts course at Columbia University, intent on a career as an artist, and supported himself by working as a waiter. He also took a course in public speaking at the Lennox Hill Settlement House and gradually became involved in their stage plays. A variety of amateur experiences lead to him being accepted as a chorus boy in the Broadway production *Pitter Patter* in 1920, and he eked out a living as a bit-part actor, singer, and vaudevillian until he made a good impression with his performance in Maxwell Anderson's *Outside Looking In* in 1925. Five years later, after a middling amount of success in various dramas and musicals, Cagney was cast in *Penny Arcade* and taken to Hollywood after its short run to appear in the film version. In his first year in the movies he played supporting roles in four other pictures and then, in 1931, made his breakthrough as *The Public Enemy*. From then on it was a matter of three and four Cagney pictures every year, culminating in his Oscar-winning performance as the celebrated song-and-dance man George M. Cohan in *Yankee Doodle Dandy* in 1942. It was at this pinnacle of success that Cagney decided to end his long association with Warner Bros., with whom he had constantly fought for better roles and greater income, and start his own company, with brother William as his producer. Their first film was *Johnny Come Lately* (1943), a genial

account of the Louis Bromfield novel *McLeod's Folly*, but it was a far cry from *Yankee Doodle Dandy* and did poorly at the box office.

For their next picture the Cagney brothers decided to tackle something more exciting and revert to more familiar fare. *Blood on the Sun* did much better, and even allowed Cagney to indulge his interest in judo. In previous films the public had admired his nimble boxing and his agile dancing; now they could watch his prowess in the oriental martial arts and further demonstrate that bantams are not always beaten by the big boys.

The Cagney image of the self-styled, tough but good-hearted, exceedingly independent loner is well in evidence in *Blood on the Sun*. The setting is Tokyo (filmed entirely within the Samuel Goldwyn Studios in Hollywood) in the early thirties, during the presidency of Herbert Hoover, at a time when Japanese military ambitions were already beginning to become evident. Here Cagney is Nick Condon, the American managing editor of the *Tokyo Chronicle*, an English language newspaper, whose owner (Porter Hall) becomes nervous when Condon prints an article about the plans of the prime minister, Baron Tanaka (John Emery) to rule the world. Tanaka has set out his plans in manuscript form, à la *Mein Kampf*, but he is not yet prepared to have them revealed. However, political opponents in Japan acquire the manuscript and give it to one of Condon's reporters, Ollie Miller (Wallace Ford), to publish. Before he can leave Japan, Miller and his wife (Rosemary De Camp) are murdered and the papers retrieved.

With the murder of the Millers, Condon reaffirms his intentions to tell the world about Tanaka, which results in an invitation from the cultured politician to visit him in his home and be assured of his goodwill toward the rest of the world. Condon remains unimpressed. He admits to liking the Japanese in general but, "The higher up you go, the lower grade people you meet." One of the people he meets is an elegant, beautiful half-Chinese, half-American named Iris Hilliard (Sylvia Sidney), with whom Condon is smitten. She impresses him with her idealistic talk of women's rights in China and Japan, pointing out that they have no rights whatsoever and that if they had they might have a civilizing influence upon male political arrogance. Condon begins to have doubts about her when he finds she is an acquaintance of Tanaka, but she is actually deceiving the prime minister in order to abort his ambitions. Iris is a Chinese patriot, and it is she who has possession of his manuscript. Realizing that he has been revealed and that he has thereby dishonored the emperor, Tanaka commits suicide in the traditional hara-kiri ceremony.

Others in the Tanaka camp, particularly Colonel Tojo

Cagney starts to uncover the plot...
...and battles the secret-police officer
(Jack Halloran).

(Robert Armstrong) of the secret police, resolve to carry on his plans for world conquest and attempt to recapture the manuscript. While Condon fights and kills police Captain Oshima (Jack Halloran), Iris escapes Japan with it. Condon then makes his way to the American Embassy but is ambushed by police and almost killed. When they find that he does not have the manuscript, the police allow the wounded Condon to make his way into the embassy. They try to convince him that it was all a mistake, and that they should all forget their indiscretions. Condon, of course, has no intention of letting it be forgotten.

Blood on the Sun was a peculiar film to be released in June of 1945, with victory over Japan within obvious reach. Had it been released prior to the attack on Pearl Harbor its warning about

Japanese military-industrial ambitions might have had some impact. Revelations of such plans as those of Baron Tanaka had made plain Japan's expansionist intentions, and yet they were virtually ignored. In view of Hollywood's pro-British sympathies and the many films made about Nazi ambitions and infiltrations prior to America's entry into the war against Germany, it is astounding that the movie producers displayed almost no interest in what was taking place in the Orient. *Blood on the Sun* was therefore something of a curiosity item, and its after-the-fact story had to rely on the appeal of intrigue in an exotic setting to draw its audience. Removed from that setting, it is simply a good spy yarn, fleshed out with melodrama and action, and leaning very heavily on the presence of its star.

Blood on the Sun is far from the best of Cagney, but it does present a refinement of the characterization he had honed all through his years on the screen. The image – even when playing the gangsters – is that of the individual, the man who goes his own way and lives by his own code, the feisty little fellow who doesn't like to take orders but usually does – in his own style. In that sense, James Cagney was, and is, a unique figure in Hollywood lore and a distinct idealization of the American Man.

Frank Puglia turning over the evidence of Japan's imperial plans to Sidney and Cagney.

111

Irving Bacon, Grant, Ralph Bellamy, and
Russell: things are not what they seem.

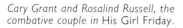

Cary Grant and Rosalind Russell, the
combative couple in His Girl Friday.

SIX

LIBERATED
AND BEAUTIFUL

he fact that the women's liberation movement gained most of its momentum and influence in the United States is surprising to people in other lands. To them – and it is an image largely fostered by Hollywood – American women have always been liberated. And well off. The European and oriental audiences during Hollywood's Golden Age would have been amazed to learn that the ladies in the land that produced the likes of Rosalind Russell, Carole Lombard, Barbara Stanwyck, et al., were in need of aid in maintaining equal rights. The likes of Russell, Lombard, and Stanwyck never, of course, needed organized help in reaching fame and fortune. Indeed the image they projected was one of strength. In *Lady of Burlesque* Stanwyck is very much the survivor, very much her own person. In *Swing High, Swing Low*, Lombard is a stronger and more courageous human than the man she loves, and in *His Girl Friday* Russell matches her wily, hard-driving male vis-à-vis step by step. None of these lovely ladies could ever be described as a shrinking violet. They are very definitely American women.

His Girl Friday brought together three of the most distinct individuals in the American cinema – Cary Grant, Rosalind Russell and Howard Hawks. The idea of doing the film was Hawks's, who one evening at a gathering at his home took out the script of *The Front Page*, the greatly successful play by Ben

113

Hecht and Charles MacArthur, and asked a woman guest to read the part of the reporter, Hildy Johnson, to his reading of the editor, Walter Burns. In the 1931 filming, directed by Lewis Milestone, Pat O'Brien had played the ace reporter and Adolphe Menjou the conniving, fast-talking editor. It occurred to Hawks that the idea of a woman playing Hildy Johnson gave the play an additional quality; Columbia chieftain Harry Cohn agreed and suggested Rosalind Russell, after his contract star Jean Arthur turned it down. For the role of Burns there was never any other actor in Hawks's mind. He had directed Cary Grant in *Bringing Up Baby* (1938) and *Only Angels Have Wings* (1939) and knew that Grant's brash charm and ability to deliver fast, glib dialogue was precisely what was needed for the part of the unscrupulous editor, especially since the part as rewritten called for the editor to be the ex-husband of the reporter he wants back on his team. Hawks asked Ben Hecht how he felt about the change of sex for Hildy Johnson, and Hecht agreed it was a stroke of genius.

Cary Grant was born in England in January of 1904 but his image, despite the mid-Atlantic accent, is largely American. Born Alexander Archibald Leach of poor circumstances, he was sent at the age of ten, when his mother died, to a boarding school, from which he ran away three years later. He joined a troupe of itinerant acrobats, but he was found by his father a month later and sent back to school. However, two years later he ran away

again and rejoined the same troupe, of which he now became an apprentice and learned about dancing, stilt-walking, tumbling, and the rudiments of comedy. In 1920 the troupe played New York and afterwards sixteen-year-old Archie decided to stay in America. He did a variety of jobs, including being a stilt-walker in a Coney Island amusement park and appearing in small, traveling vaudeville companies. In 1923 he returned to London to appear in stage musicals, which eventually brought him back to New York. In 1927 he was a juvenile lead in *The Golden Dawn*, and in the next four years he slowly built up a reputation as a reliable young actor-singer. In late 1931 he set out with the idea of trying the movies and crossed the country in a second-hand car. A director at Paramount hired him to play opposite an actress he was testing; the actress did not pass the test but Archie's looks and personality won him an offer to stay with the studio – once they had found a new name for him.

In 1932 Cary Grant appeared in no less than seven Paramount pictures, and in the following thirty years he would average two or three films a year and become a Hollywood giant. *His Girl Friday* was his thirty-fifth movie. For Rosalind Russell it

The newspaper office,
à la Hollywood.

was film number twenty-one. Four years younger than Grant, she was born of a good middle-class family in Waterbury, Connecticut, of a father who had been a college athlete and later a prominent trial lawyer. His views on physical fitness led his daughter to become a tomboy, and a very lively one at that. She was a curious, energetic girl, and she would grow up into that kind of woman. From college she went to the American Academy of Dramatic Art in New York, and afterwards, with her good looks, well-bred manner, and fine speaking voice – her father was also a stickler about diction – she was able to get work in stock companies. She first appeared on Broadway in *The Garrick Gaities of 1930*. There were a number of offers of screen tests in the next few years but, ever independent, she declined them until she liked the one offered by Universal in 1934. But she refused to take the test in New York and demanded that Universal shoot it in Hollywood and pay all her expenses. They did, but while they were working out the terms of her contract she was tested by MGM, who made a better offer, which she accepted. It was characteristic of Rosalind Russell that she would enter the movies on her own terms. At twenty-six she had but a small reputation as an actress but she knew what she wanted. That sense of self-assurance would mark her image all through

her film career.

In her first dozen pictures Rosalind Russell played second leads, but she was loaned to Columbia in 1936 for the title role in *Craig's Wife*, the success of which made MGM more concerned about the next assignment. This turned out to be *Night Must Fall*, co-starring her with Robert Montgomery in a classic murder mystery. But acclaim as an actress did not really come until she appeared in George Cukor's *The Women* in 1939, which for the first time allowed her to reveal her talent for comedy and her odd ability to combine the hoyden with the aristocrat. It set the Rosalind Russell image – a distinctly American image of the modern woman, loving but fully capable of handling men, and not much in need of the later liberation movement. It was her playing in *The Women* that convinced Cohn, and later Hawks, that she was the right choice for *His Girl Friday*. And her attire in this picture – the pin-striped suit with the padded shoulders – would set her sartorial style in the films that followed, films in which she was invariably a coldly efficient businesswoman but always with a warm heart and a sense of humor.

Hildy Johnson is just such a woman, a top-notch reporter who has just divorced her boss, Walter Burns, the editor of the *Morning Star* and a man who would do almost anything to get a

115

The bridegroom-to-be (Bellamy) starts to have his doubts...

...and so does the bride-to-be.

116

On the set with director Howard Hawks.

story for his paper. He is a tough veteran of the crazy world of journalism, and when she visits him after her return from Reno it is to tell him she is getting married again – to a nice fellow named Bruce Baldwin (Ralph Bellamy), who is an insurance salesman from Albany, New York, where Hildy looks forward to a quiet life, far removed from Burns's mad-house antics. But she has arrived at a time when he badly needs her talent to cover the story of a murderer, Earl Williams (John Qualen), who is set to go to the electric chair while maintaining his innocence. Burns knows Hildy is the only reporter who can get the real flavor out of a story like that, and he cajoles, badgers, and maneuvers her into taking the job – but for just this one assignment, it is understood. Hildy does all that is expected of her, even interviewing the condemned man in his cell. When he escapes she hides him in her roll-top desk in her office. All the while Burns does his best to sabotage her romance with the nice insurance salesman from Albany and convince her that she has no place in that sort of quiet life. She has printer's ink in her blood, and besides, he constantly says, she is his kind of girl. Eventually Walter Burns gets his ex-wife and reporter back, as well as getting the story he needs. He also comes close to being thrown in jail himself. The escaped man is recaptured by the sheriff (Gene Lockhart) in the press room, and Burns and Hildy are then arrested for obstructing justice. But they are released when

it comes to light that the sheriff and the mayor (Clarence Kolb) are in cahoots to bribe the messenger from the governor in order to stop the reprieve from being delivered in time. The condemned man is saved, and the sheriff and the mayor lose their positions. Hildy agrees to remarry Burns and go with him on a honeymoon to Niagara – but another story turns up and the honeymoon has to be delayed. The job comes first, but Hildy knows it is her way of life, and she loves it.

His Girl Friday is yet another example of a film comedy that could not be the product of any country other than the United States. The speed with which Howard Hawks moved Cary Grant and Rosalind Russell through their roles and the rapidity of the dialogue mark it as peculiarly American. So too is the film's rather caustic view of the human animal; Hecht and MacArthur were not shedding a kindly light on the more opportunistic aspects of American journalism or the way local politicians use human grief for their own advantage. These are, of course, universal traits but the style with which Hawks illuminates them is uniquely American. The pacing, the brashness of Grant's Walter Burns, the smart but vulnerable Hildy Johnson of Rosalind Russell, the wisecracks, the glib reporters, and the attitude that journalism is a competitive business – all this is clearly a product of Hollywood. The fourth estate has had its knuckles well rapped on the American screen.

Fred MacMurray and Carole Lombard
in Swing High, Swing Low.

MacMurray and Lombard with a very young Anthony Quinn, in those days so often cast as a gigolo.

She was very much an American actress. It is difficult to think of Carole Lombard as a European or an English-woman. She was an intriguing mixture of classiness and earthi-ness, and she had such a talent for light comedy that the critics sometimes referred to her as a comedienne. But Lombard was far more than that. Her style ranged from poignant to raucous, and with it all she was beautiful. She was liberated long before it was fashionable and dealt with men, both on screen and off, in a direct manner. In 1928 Joseph P. Kennedy, then head of Pathé Pictures, told her he would use her if she lost some weight. She accepted the advice but on the way out of his office said, "You're not so skinny yourself." Lombard was blunt spoken and a practical joker but she was also lovable. In short, she was extraordinary. Bing Crosby, who co-starred with her in *We're Not Dressing* (1934), recalled, "The electricians, carpenters, and prop men all adored her because she was so regular, so devoid of temperament and show boating. The fact that she could make us think of her as being a good guy rather than a sexy mamma is one of those unbelievable manifestations impossible to explain."

Carole Lombard was born in Indiana in October of 1908 and moved with her family to Los Angeles when she was a child. Director Alan Dwan spotted her when she was thirteen and gave her a small part in one of his pictures, but four years went by before she got another chance to be in the movies. Her career began in 1925, playing in westerns and Mack Sennett comedies, but her contract with Pathé – Kennedy was as good as his word – put her into full-time work as a leading player.

Lombard's career moved into orbit when Paramount cast her opposite Charles "Buddy" Rogers in *Safety in Numbers* in 1931, and afterwards signed her to a seven-year contract. Over the next few years she gradually emerged as a lady with her own style, a slinky blonde adept at wisecracks and hiding her soft heart behind a somewhat brash manner. In 1934 she delighted audiences with her portrayal of the temperamental movie star who stands up to tyrannical director John Barrymore in *Twentieth Century*, after which Barrymore said, "She is perhaps the greatest actress I ever worked with." With her performance two years later opposite William Powell in *My Man Godfrey* there was no

119

Lombard and MacMurray performing in a Panama City cabaret.

doubt in anyone's mind that she was a luminary in Hollywood life.

In 1936 Lombard did the first of four appearances with Fred MacMurray – *Hands Across the Table*. MacMurray was the same age as Lombard and they made a pleasing team. He was hired by Paramount in 1934 and immediately used as a leading man in light comedies, which would be the tone of his career from then on. MacMurray has always essayed the all-American nice guy – slightly bumbling, seemingly lazy, genial but determined. Only rarely was he a villain, and even though he performed with distinction as a cold-blooded cad in *Double Indemnity* (1944), it did not alter his lingering image as the good-looking "man next door" who somehow gets into odd situations and comically muddles through. Sometimes MacMurray was able to get parts that suggested, rather poignantly, that there was pain beneath the glib surface. This was the case in *Swing High, Swing Low*, his second film with Lombard.

120

Dorothy Lamour, the nightclub chanteuse in love with MacMurray, the man she cannot have.

As *Swing High, Swing Low* opens both stars appear to be their usual selves as they banter with wisecracks – he the aggressor on the make and she the girl who has heard it all before. The scene is the Panama Canal, as Maggie looks out the porthole of her cabin and comes to the attention of a U.S. Army sentry, Skid Johnson (MacMurray). He tells her it is the last day of his service and invites her to celebrate with him the evening. She allows that maybe she will turn up. She does, in the company of her friend Ella (Jean Dixon) and meets Skid and his hypochondriacal buddy Harry (Charles Butterworth). The bantering between Skid and Maggie is a mask for the real attraction they have for one another, and it also becomes apparent that they are both different from the impression they give. Maggie is softer and more compassionate, and Skid is a weaker and more disturbed man than she had first thought.

In a cabaret during their first date, Skid picks up a trumpet and reveals himself to be a talented musician, and she becomes as smitten with him as he obviously is with her. When a local gigolo (Anthony Quinn) tries to pick her up, Skid comes to the rescue and because of the damage done in the inevitable brawl both he and Maggie are put in jail for a night. By the next morning Maggie has decided to stay with him and not resume her journey. She finds him to be a man in need of help, and she gives him the support that pulls him out of his lax ways. She is a singer, and she joins with him to do an act after she manages to get him a job in a nightclub. Together they do a song called "I Feel a Call to Arms," and it becomes *their* song.

The negative forces in Skid's character make life unsettling for Maggie. She marries him but cannot halt his wandering attentions. Skid falls for a dark-haired singer, Anita (Dorothy Lamour), and goes with her to New York when Anita promises to help him get into the big money. He does well, and when

Maggie turns up to ask for a divorce he tells her he doesn't care. But inwardly he is crumbling from the lack of strength in his character. He gets drunk and keeps drinking until his career and his health are ruined. He tries to get back in the army but they reject him. Skid gets a chance to play in a radio broadcast, but he is so weak he can barely stand up. Maggie, who still cares, appears at the studio and literally supports him as he plays. He plays their song and she sings along with him, and the film ends on a note of possible hope for Skid and Maggie.

The poignancy of *Swing High, Swing Low* rests with the playing of Lombard and MacMurray but the unseen force is that of director Mitchell Leisen, who started as a costume designer and a set decorator with Paramount in 1919 and spent most of his career with that studio. He began directing in 1933 and two years later directed Lombard and MacMurray in *Hands Across the Table*. He therefore knew they were the right talents for *Swing High, Swing Low*, a film that demanded more of its actors than first appearances suggested. Leisen was a gentleman of taste, and this combined with his background as an artist gave his pictures a high style, especially in terms of visual elegance. That elegance is very evident in his *Lady in the Dark* (1944), *Frenchman's Creek* (1944), and *To Each His Own* (1946). And it is Leisen's subtle touches that give *Swing High, Swing Low* qualities it might not otherwise have had. Certainly it presents Carole Lombard to great advantage, as a truly beautiful, sensitive, caring woman.

Carole Lombard went on to please her public with films like *Nothing Sacred* (1937), *Made For Each Other* (1939), and finally *To Be or Not To Be* (1942). She married Clark Gable in 1939 and settled down to a happy marriage, and gave it all the attention she could, even to sacrificing her own career. The happiness came to a shocking end in early 1942 when she was killed in a plane crash while touring the country to sell war bonds. No actress since then has come close to filling the void she left.

Swing High, Swing Low was Dorothy Lamour's second film, following her colorful debut in *The Jungle Princess*. In his book *Hollywood Director: The Career of Mitchell Leisen*, David Chierichetti discussed Carole Lombard with Dorothy Lamour: "I was still very new to the game and being such a big fan of Carole's I was completely in awe. On our first scene together, I blew my lines over and over. Carole always knew her lines perfectly, but she began to blow them on purpose just so I wouldn't feel so bad. Any star who will do that for a newcomer has got to be the greatest, and Carole really was wonderful. She made me feel right at home....I have never known anybody as kind and generous as Carole."

(Left)
Lombard auditioning a song in New York with Jean Dixon, Charles Butterworth, and MacMurray.

Lombard and MacMurray rehearsing the final scene.

123

Barbara Stanwyck in Lady of Burlesque, 1942

"I have never worked with an actress who was more co-operative, less temperamental, and a better workman, to use my term of highest compliment, than Barbara Stanwyck. I have directed, and enjoyed working with, many fine actresses, some of whom are also good workmen; but when I count over those of whom my memories are unmarred by any unpleasant recollection of friction on the set, or unwillingness to do whatever the role required, or squalls of temperament or temper, Barbara's name is the first that comes to mind, as one on whom a director can always count to do her work with all her heart."

So said Cecil B. DeMille, one of the most imperial of all Hollywood directors. His opinion of Barbara Stanwyck is in line with that of almost every director, actor, or technician who has worked with her during the course of a film career that started in 1927. In the following thirty years she made eighty films – a productivity and longevity that is rare among actresses. In 1957, at the age of fifty, she found, as did all female stars, that parts were no longer plentiful. Male stars could go on and on; the ladies had to settle for semiretirement and cameo roles. It is an injustice that points up the continuing fact that life in the entertainment industry is harder for women than it is for men.

She was born Ruby Stevens in Brooklyn, and by the age of four she was an orphan. The last of five children, she went to live with her sister Mildred, who was a chorus girl in musicals and traveled frequently, at which times Ruby was boarded with friends. The experience caused her to become a lonely child, and she spent as much time as she could going to the movies to enjoy the fantasies. One of her sister's friends was a vaudevillian, and he taught Ruby how to dance. By the age of fifteen she was good enough to be hired by Earl Lindsay, the director of New York's Strand Roof, and from there she got engagements in various nightclubs. Within a year she also appeared as a chorus girl in *The Ziegfeld Follies of 1922* and later went on the road with it. There were many small parts until her break in 1926 when she played the lead, the role of a cabaret dancer, in *The Noose*, which ran on Broadway for nine months and caused her to receive her first offers from the film people. The only thing producer Willard Mack didn't like about Ruby Stevens was her name. A new name dawned upon him as he looked at a poster hanging in the Belasco Theatre: Jane Stanwyck in *Barbara Frietchie*.

Barbara Stanwyck did a small role in a silent film made in New York in 1927, *Broadway Nights*, but she regards her real movie debut as the sound film *The Locked Door*, made two years later. Frank Capra came into her life the next year when he hired her for *Ladies of Leisure*. He also hired her for *The Miracle Woman* and *Forbidden*. Consequently, when he called her about

. . . and in a publicity still a decade earlier.

How to hide a little cash: Stanwyck and Michael O'Shea.

Meet John Doe, her reaction was exactly the same as Gary Cooper's – she didn't even want to see a script.

By the mid-thirties Barbara Stanwyck was a star of the first magnitude, with hits like *Annie Oakley*, *Banjo on My Knee*, and *Stella Dallas*. By the forties she had become an expert screen actress with a very definite image. It was a slyly attractive image, suggestive of sex appeal but never blatant and always of a woman in command of the situation. It was very much an American image, that of a lady who can make her own way in the world, with or without male help. She hit her stride with Preston Sturges's *The Lady Eve* in 1941 as a lovely confidence trickster who handles Henry Fonda like a vacuum cleaner handles dust. It was followed by her portrayal of the tough newspaper lady in *Meet John Doe* and any number of strong-minded women, some villainous, as in *Double Indemnity* (1944) and *The Strange Love of Martha Ivers* (1946), but more often than not a good woman, as in *My Reputation* (1946) and *Sorry, Wrong Number* (1948). But no matter the personality of the part, it was never that of a weak woman.

In 1943 she welcomed the opportunity to do something a little different. The elegant, celebrated stripteaser, Gypsy Rose Lee, whose act was always more verbal than physical and quite sedate by later standards, wrote a novel called *The G-String Murders*, which producer Hunt Stromberg believed would make an excellent film. He found, however, that few among the public knew what a G-string was, and he retitled it *Lady of Burlesque*. The strictures of 1943 censorship also required him to tone down the earthiness of the setting and avoid any graphic filming of bumps and grinds. Stanwyck was able to display some of the knowledge she had learned of vaudeville in her youth, and surprised her fans with her singing of "Take It Off the E-String, Play It on the G-String," together with cartwheels, splits, and sexy patter.

Lady of Burlesque is a well-mounted and affectionate look at a uniquely American form of show business, the girly-girly branch of vaudeville, although the confines of censorship limited the vulgarity that was an essential part of burlesque. The raunchy humor had to be toned down, and the censors allowed no nudity. The real values of the film are the observations which Gypsy Rose Lee made of her profession and its people, which James Gunn carried over into his screenplay and which director William Wellman conveyed with his probings into the dingy dressing rooms and the backstage relationships. Somehow Wellman and his writer managed to combine cynicism with sentiment and reveal the feelings beneath the hard, flashy surface of the

Burlesque in action: Stanwyck, Frank Fenton, and O'Shea.

J. Edward Bromberg, the company manager, and his cast.

strippers and the comics, the pathos under the rough, rowdy camaraderie.

The lady of the title is Dixie Daisy (Stanwyck), who is in the process of being promoted to stardom by her employer, S.B. Foss (J. Edward Bromberg) as he opens his new show in a former opera house. There are many jealousies among the girls but none strong enough to suggest a motive for the killing of one of them in her dressing room, strangled with her own G-string (the thin belt strippers use to cover the pubic area). The police move in and become as amused as they are bewildered by the girls and the comics, who are all protective of one another. The situation worsens when another stripper is found dead, also done in by a G-string. Dixie finds herself romanced by the show's top comic, Biff Brannigan (Michael O'Shea) and gradually responds to the sincerity he conceals under his brash manner. Together Dixie and Biff solve the murders and turn in the culprit.

Lady of Burlesque is one of the few films to delve into the theatre of bumps-and-grinds. If made today it would be a lot more candid, but in 1943 it was necessary for the producers to suggest more than they could reveal, which is in itself an art. William Wellman, a director who always moved his material at a neat clip, captured the salty atmosphere of burlesque and the character of its backstage milieu. But the film's major asset is its star. Barbara Stanwyck, one of the most warmly regarded women in Hollywood, here threw herself with a great sense of bravura into the role of the stripper, strutting on stage and delivering her lines like a real trouper – as indeed she was. In more than eighty movies there was never such a thing as a disappointing Barbara Stanwyck performance.

Stanwyck and O'Shea.

Ronald Reagan as George Armstrong Custer and Errol Flynn as Jeb Stuart on duty at Fort Leavenworth, Kansas, 1854, in Santa Fe Trail.

SEVEN

THE WEST THAT NEVER WAS

The western is a form of American mythology. Of all the kinds of American life depicted on the screen it is the most exciting and the least accurate. It began in 1903 with *The Great Train Robbery*, and in the first years of its life the western was a spillover from the real West. Many of the cowboys and the extras in those early films were men who found it much more profitable and far easier to work in westerns than labor on cattle and horse ranches. Some of them were actually men who had escaped the law in their own states and who no doubt helped the writers with ideas for plots and characters. That life for most people in the real West was hard and dull is beside the point. The point of the western is entertainment, and as such it is a broad canvas. Almost any story can be set in the West, and it can be enlivened with action, with scenery, and with clear-cut values. The western comfortably belongs to the past and if the images and notions are false, who cares? It is easy to watch Errol Flynn and Ronald Reagan as dashing cavalrymen fighting wars that no longer have to be fought. And even easier to believe there were

once stalwart individuals out West who looked like Randolph Scott and John Wayne.

Ronald Reagan refers to himself in the early years of his film career as the "Errol Flynn of the B pictures." Reagan was signed by Warner Bros. in 1937 (he was twenty-six at the time) after having made a name for himself as a radio sports commentator. For the first four years of his busy contract he was either the lead in minor movies or a supporting player in major ones. In the B pictures he was more often than not a courageous newspaper reporter investigating crimes or a secret service operator fighting espionage. It wasn't until Warners cast him in *Knute Rockne – All American* (1940) as the legendary football player George Gipp that the public had a chance to observe Reagan as an actor of talent.

Errol Flynn, a Tasmanian whose adventures are now very well documented in several books, was given a contract by Warners in 1935 and reached superstardom within a year as the dashing Captain Blood. Because of his refined British speech and manner Flynn was mostly cast in historical yarns with a British setting. In 1939, in an obvious effort to widen his horizons,

Warners cast Flynn in an epic western, *Dodge City*. Somewhat to his own surprise he did well in the Wild West and after several more westerns Flynn referred to himself as "the rich man's Roy Rogers." He also found himself gradually being eased by Warners out of the pages of British history and into those of America. His first portrayal of an American historical character was James Ewell Brown Stuart (1833–1864), the brilliant cavalry commander of the Confederacy and one of its most colorful cavaliers.

However, in casting Flynn as Jeb Stuart his employers required from him nothing in the way of accuracy. *Santa Fe Trail* did not even touch upon Stuart's claim to fame, his success in the Civil War, but dealt with his involvement as a U.S. Army cavalry lieutenant in the campaign against abolitionist John Brown in the years just before the war. Warners decided to team Flynn with Ronald Reagan, giving Reagan the role of George Armstrong Custer and making believe that the two graduated from West Point in the same year (1854) and became friends. In point of fact Custer did not graduate until 1861 and never met Stuart, although he would become very aware of him during the war.

Custer's Michigan Brigade was part of the force used by Philip Sheridan at the battle of Yellow Tavern, in which Stuart was killed.

Santa Fe Trail stands as one of Hollywood's most curious forays into American history. It looks like a western and yet it isn't. It has nothing to do with wagon trains and pioneers and never gets any further west than Kansas. It doesn't even have much to do with the Santa Fe Trail. Instead it deals with the army's attempts to track down John Brown and stop his abolitionist crusade in Kansas. In doing this the film vacillates politically – from being conservative in its support of government

Reagan, Alan Hale, and Flynn capture one of John Brown's sons (Gene Reynolds).

The Washington ball: Flynn, Olivia De Havilland, Susan Peters, and Reagan.

(Left)
West Point, the commandant with cadets: Moroni Olsen, Frank Wilcox, David Bruce, George Haywood, Reagan, Flynn, William Lundigan, and William Marshall.

Raymond Massey as John Brown captured by Flynn.

and army policies, and liberal in viewing the efforts of a brave man to free the slaves. As played by Raymond Massey, Brown appears as demented as he is dedicated, and when he is hung at the conclusion of the film an army officer intones, "So perish all such enemies of the Union," a view which becomes puzzling when it is realized that Brown was trying to do what Lincoln did with such acclaim a few years later.

But the oddities of *Santa Fe Trail* do not end with its convoluted views of history. For reasons of his own, scenarist Robert Buckner chose to take a number of the most famous names in military annals and lump them together as comrades. The film opens at West Point in 1854 and presents Stuart as about to graduate and receive his commission. But in his class also are Custer, Philip Sheridan, James Longstreet, George Pickett, and James Hood (all Civil War generals), none of whom graduated that year. So as a history lesson *Santa Fe Trail* is highly dubious stuff. It can only be looked upon as an interesting departure point for a study of John Brown, Jeb Stuart, et al., and as a first-class piece of film making in the adventure genre. Warners allotted a solid budget and assigned it to director Michael Curtiz, who was a master with action pictures. He truly knew how to make a movie move and how to construct it with mounting excitement, as did veteran composer Max Steiner, whose full-blooded score pulsates and generously supports most of the two-hour running time. Along with the photography and the editing, *Santa Fe Trail* is a textbook example of an action epic, and with Flynn and Reagan as storybook cavalrymen, it is good fun to watch.

According to Buckner's screenplay, Stuart and Custer are assigned to the Second U.S. Cavalry, stationed at Fort Leavenworth, Kansas. There they both fall in love with Kit Halliday (Olivia De Havilland), the daughter of a frontier businessman (Henry O'Neill). The job of patrolling the frontier brings them into conflict with John Brown, his family, and his followers. In his attempts to free the slaves, Brown causes bloodshed and bitterness as people either side with him or against him. To make his campaigns more tactical Brown hires a cashiered West Point cadet, Rader (Van Heflin), but it is this same ex-cadet who, presumably in the name of patriotism but more likely because Brown never paid him, informs on Brown and reports his movements to the army. When Brown takes over the strategic town of Harpers Ferry, Virginia, and seizes its large armory, an army force under the command of Colonel Robert E. Lee (Moroni Olsen) – historically correct – is sent to engage him. Stuart, under white flag, is ordered to confer with Brown – also

The hanging of John Brown, 1859.

true – but when the fanatical abolitionist, calling for help from God, refuses to surrender he is attacked and his forces beaten. He is tried for treason and hung. When last seen Stuart and Custer are on a train, with Stuart in the process of being married, as the sound track closes with Steiner's dramatic variations on "John Brown's Body."

As entertainment *Santa Fe Trail* is grade A material; as a history lesson it is confusing and dubious. As a piece of film making in the grand tradition, it offers many memorable images. The scenes at West Point are well mounted, with good points made in favor of old-fashioned military glory as cavalry cadets go through their paces and Secretary of War Jefferson Davis (Erville Alderson) addresses the graduating class and reminds them of their duty and their honor as soldiers. Raymond Massey, darkly and dramatically lit by the brilliant Sol Polito, conveys the fierce dedication of Brown as he rallies his followers and shepherds the frightened blacks. And director Curtiz mounts his action

sequences with swift strokes and pacing; his cameras track the chase of Brown's wagon train by the cavalry, and they dart back and forth as Flynn later fights his way in and out of a burning barn. Those same cameras capture the urgency of military conferences and the grace of a handsome military ball in Washington. But most of all they reveal the complicated and exciting movements in the battle at Harpers Ferry and the final takeover by the army of the armory. Cannons roar, soldiers charge, shells tear jagged holes in the armory, the cavalrymen whip up dust as they ride, men on both sides fight and fall, and finally the battering rams smash down the doors and the soldiers quell the remainder of Brown's followers. All of it is deftly photographed, edited, performed, and scored under the command of Michael Curtiz, a man with a reputation for being a tough, hard workhorse. Had he not been a film director he might well have been a military tactician, most probably of the old Prussian school.

135

Randolph Scott, sheriff of
Abilene Town...
...and his dance-hall girl
friend, Ann Dvorak.

When David O. Selznick was casting *Gone With the Wind* fans of various stars deluged him with suggestions for the principal roles. The actor the public most seemed to want for Ashley Wilkes was Randolph Scott, who might have got the part had not Selznick sold himself on the idea that Leslie Howard was an actor with a higher international reputation than Scott, and therefore of greater value. It is true that in 1938 Scott's esteem was not the equal of Howard's, but the consensus is that Howard's playing of Wilkes is the weakest of the main parts in *GWTW*. Howard himself made no secret of his disdain for the role and said he did it only for money. It remains conjecture how well Randolph Scott would have done. It is highly likely he would have been excellent and that the role would have altered the course of his career. Greatly in his favor was the fact that Scott is himself a southern gentleman and would have had to change nothing about his accent or his bearing to seem exactly like the Ashley whom Margaret Mitchell painted with her words. Scott had actually played a Wilkes-like part in Paramount's *So Red the Rose* (1936), in which he was a southern gentleman who loves plantation owner Margaret Sullavan, fights for the Confederacy, and returns to rebuild the South. Sadly, *So Red the Rose* was a financial disaster and its failure probably turned Selznick off of associating Scott with the similar role of Ashley Wilkes. If so, it is regrettable.

Randolph Scott was born in Roanoke, Virginia, in January of 1903 and is a descendant of the first settlers in that state. His mother was the daughter of an old-guard North Carolina family; she married George G. Scott, a textile engineer, and their son was educated at a number of private schools before attending Georgia Tech, where a back injury prevented him from attaining his goal of becoming an all-American football player. The injury was severe enough that the damage was permanent and caused him to be turned down for military service in the Second World War. Scott spent the last two years of his schooling at the University of North Carolina and studied toward entering his father's line of work. He afterwards began an apprenticeship with his father's textile company but shocked both his parents with his apparent interest in the theatre. His father's advice was to get it out of his system by trying it and then returning to textiles, and he gave him a letter of introduction to the only man Scott senior knew with any connection in the entertainment business – Howard Hughes in Los Angeles.

Scott managed to see the elusive Howard Hughes, who arranged for him to get work as an extra in a George O'Brien western, *Sharp Shooters*, in 1928. The experience was enough for

137

Edgar Buchanan comes to the aid of a sheriff much in need of it...
...but he doesn't have as much luck playing cards with the sheriff.

Scott to decide that the movies and not the theatre was the line he should pursue. To learn about acting, of which he obviously knew nothing, he attended the Pasadena Community Theatre for two years, with odd jobs on the side. One of those jobs was coaching Gary Cooper in a Virginia accent for *The Virginian*. Scott's performance in the play *Under a Virginia Moon* at the Vine Street Theatre in Hollywood in 1932 resulted in several offers for screen tests and he accepted the one from Paramount. After a couple of small parts they decided to give him the lead in a western, *Wild Horse Mesa*, a decision that would have a great influence on his movie career. Scott had never been a cowboy, but he loved horses and had ridden in fox hunts in Virginia as a youngster. *Wild Horse Mesa* proved him to be an idealization of the fictional western hero, and Paramount had him do a half dozen more westerns in the next two years. In the years that followed Scott did a variety of films – drawing room comedies, musicals, adventure yarns, and war movies – but it was in westerns that he seemed perfectly at ease. By the time he appeared in *Abilene Town*, his fiftieth film, he had settled for the idea of making the western his specialty from then on. After *Abilene Town* in 1946 Scott went on to make another forty movies, all but two of them westerns. He retired in 1962, after thirty very busy years before the cameras.

Abilene Town was among the first attempts to paint the West with a little more accuracy than had been the case in Hollywood until that time. Producer Jules Levey bought the rights to Ernest Haycox's novel *Trail Town* but changed the title in order to take advantage of the fact that Abilene, Kansas, the point to which the Texas ranchers drove their cattle to meet the railroad, was the home town of Dwight D. Eisenhower. In order to use the name of the town Levey had to seek permission from the mayor, who agreed provided Levey start his movie with some shots of present day Abilene and an explanation that it was nothing like the wild place Haycox wrote about in his popular novel.

Abilene Town concerns that greatly popular period of western history, the decade following the Civil War, when the cattle business boomed with the coming of the railroads and settlers poured into the Great Plains, mostly to become farmers, and where they often conflicted with the cattle interests. The film focuses on the problems of 1870, with Abilene swamped with the money brought by the Texas drovers as they sold their cattle to brokers, who then put the meat on railcars bound for the East. It is a time when the main street of Abilene was a division between good and bad. It is called Texas Street. On the one side are the saloons and houses of pleasure, frequented by

The sheriff and his deputies ride out of town, a classic western scene.

fun-seeking cowboys, and on the other side are the stores and businesses catering to the settlers. The town marshall, Dan Mitchell (Scott), has to work both sides of the street and keep order. His romantic interests are also divided by the street – between Rita (Ann Dvorak), a dance hall queen, and Sherry (Rhonda Fleming), the lovely young daughter of a merchant. Eventually he comes to realize that the dancer is a girl with a heart of gold and the right one for him.

The plot lines of *Abilene Town* were familiar long before 1946, and they have become more so since. In dealing with this, or any western, the criteria are style and quality of production. Randolph Scott is the primary quality in this film, as a marshall who knows how to balance the conflicting elements of the wild times, who knows the value of the cattle herds in the economy of the town but also knows that the future belongs with the settlers. As in many other westerns, he is the figure of quiet authority and courage who had to seek out the criminal factors and eradicate them, usually with a gun in his hand. The figure is

one of the major clichés in the annals of American film, but it is to Scott's credit that the figure is admirable and credible. And it is to the credit of the veteran director Edwin L. Marin that the action in *Abilene Town* is both sensible and exciting. The saloon brawls, the gun play in the street, and especially the cattle stampede give the film its brisk pacing. When such action is not sensibly staged it becomes boring. Marin also knew how to place the musical segments, well delivered by Ann Dvorak, and the comedy, most of it coming from Edgar Buchanan as a deputy with a great dislike for danger.

Randolph Scott liked working with Edwin L. Marin and did seven more films with him. In 1949 Scott and producer Nat Holt formed their own company and specialized in westerns, beginning with the admirable *Canadian Pacific*, which Marin directed. Scott also started another company with producer Harry Joe Brown to do more westerns. All the films, especially the seven directed by the remarkable Budd Boetticher, are head and shoulders above the average run of westerns, and they have

Jack Lambert, villain no more, thanks to Sheriff Scott.

The citizens of Abilene Town show their relief.

helped give Scott a particular niche in film history.

Ride the High Country (1962), directed by Sam Peckinpah, is among the finest of all westerns, a truly beautiful account of a pair of veteran westerners whose day has come and gone. Randolph Scott and Joel McCrea chose to make it their swan song in the movies, and they could not have chosen a better vehicle. Ironically, both Scott and McCrea were by 1962 both very wealthy men, presumably even more wealthy now, and the idea of them playing a pair of hard-up old cowboys is somewhat amusing. They had never before worked together but their careers had run parallel, starting at about the same time and ending with both of them becoming stalwart western figures, as well as greatly respected and well liked men off screen. Of Scott, Michael Curtiz, who directed him in *Virginia City* (1940), said, "Randy Scott is a complete anachronism. He's a gentleman. And so far he is the only one I've met in this business full of self-promoting sons-of-bitches."

No one has yet come up with a workable formula for what it takes to become a movie star. Obviously it takes some acting ability and intelligence, but there are hordes of talented, intelligent actors who never reach star status. The requirements remain beyond definition. The simplest explanation is to point to someone like John Wayne. But what was it about him that made him a star? He was not a particularly handsome man, and his talents cannot be described as exceptional. Critics often discounted him as an actor and certainly no one ever thought of him in terms of Laurence Olivier. And yet, think of Olivier trying to play Wayne's roles in the great John Ford westerns. He might have looked ridiculous. Wayne did not. He looked perfectly right. He was totally believable as a rancher or a drifter or a cavalry captain. If that isn't acting, what is it?

John Wayne cannot be compared with any other figure in film history. He is therefore unique. He had a presence that was all his own, and it must surely have had something to do with the character of the man himself. With time he became an American institution, and since his death he has graduated to legend. Although he played a variety of roles it was in westerns that he excelled, possibly because Americans, and people all around the world, saw him as the perfect realization of the fictional western hero. If the men of the real Wild West didn't look like John Wayne, they *should* have.

Wayne was another classic example of the American Dream – the man from the lower ranks of society, from obscurity, who makes it all the way to the top and does it by himself. His career was indeed remarkable. Wayne was in the movies for fifty years, and he enjoyed stardom longer than any other man. But more than that, he became an American image even apart from Hollywood. Wayne personified the old line, conservative, do-it-yourself working man who disliked government interference in his life. It was his great good fortune to be successful and never need the aids brought to the public by government programs. In time he was a conspicuous part of the polarization of American views – venerated by the older generation and ridiculed by the younger. But images are deceiving. Toward the end of his life Wayne became more liberal and the youngsters became more tolerant. Now his place is not merely part of film history but of American folklore.

Wayne was born in Winterset, Iowa, in May of 1908 and brought to California at the age of five. The family settled in Glendale, and Wayne did well all through his school years. His class averages were consistently good, and he excelled on the

John Wayne, the dashing badman, and Gail Russell, the beautiful Quaker girl who loves him ... and changes his ways: Angel and the Badman.

The archetypal John Wayne strides to the
showdown.

Lee Dixon is annoyed at the
change in his fellow badman.

football field. He also found enjoyment taking part in school plays. His ambition was to enter the United States Naval Academy, but he failed the tests and thereafter took a series of odd jobs before securing a scholarship at the University of Southern California. Due to his prowess as a member of the celebrated U.S.C. Trojan football team and the fact that cowboy star Tom Mix was an admirer of the team, Wayne was able to get a summer job in 1927 as a laborer at the Fox Studio. The first film to which he was assigned was *Mother Machree*. The director was John Ford, who took a liking to Wayne and allowed him to make some badly needed extra money by appearing in the picture as an extra. This was followed by other chances to perform in crowd scenes, in addition to chores lugging props around sets, and occasional opportunities to do stunts. Within a year Wayne was getting small parts and not long after his twenty-second birthday Fox took a chance and gave him the starring role in their large-scale epic western *The Big Trail*. It did not catapult Wayne to stardom. His performance was lackluster, and he was soon back to playing in B pictures, and not even leading roles. Two years later he established himself as a star of B westerns, and this would be the pattern of his career for the next seven years.

It is a peculiarity in the story of a man who would eventually attain the greatest heights of popularity that he did not find much of it in those years as a star of B westerns. He made a good living, but the Saturday matinee fans did not embrace him as they did Gene Autry and Roy Rogers. It was not until John Ford chose him to play in *Stagecoach* in 1939 that Wayne stepped out of the Hollywood sidelines and started a rapid climb as a box office champion. Ford's hunch that there was more to Wayne than even the actor himself realized proved to be true. The talent was dormant. Ford pushed, shoved, and goaded Wayne into stardom.

In 1946 John Wayne became a producer of films. He was not alone among actors in sensing that the postwar industry would change and that it was wise to have one's own company. Not unnaturally he chose to make a western as his first outing.

Wayne, Russell, and Craig Woods: the plot thickens as the ex-badman learns his adversaries are closing in.

However, *Angel and the Badman* is not a conventional western. It is far less violent than the average, and it espouses pacifism in the form of a Quaker heroine who alters the life of a gunslinger and causes him, through the process of love, to discard his gun. It was not an obvious choice for the first production, and neither was Wayne's choice of a director. He handed those important reins to writer James Edward Grant, who had never before directed. Grant, a screen writer since 1936, told Wayne that he felt his screenplay was different and that he was concerned about getting it on the screen without changes. Wayne suggested he direct it himself.

It was typical of Wayne that if he believed in people he would take chances. He would also, as a producer, hire the same actors over and over, and build up a stock company after the fashion of John Ford. Loyalty was characteristic of Wayne, although he was not an easy boss. It was also characteristic of Wayne that for his first production he would hire Harry Carey, a veteran western actor who was Wayne's idol and virtual father-confessor. No study of Wayne's screen persona and acting style can ignore the influence of Harry Carey. And it is interesting that Carey's role as the sheriff in *Angel and the Badman* is that of an unwavering moral force, a kind of spiritual conscience that nags the bedeviled gunman.

In *Angel and the Badman*, the badman is Quirt Evans (John Wayne), who has a reputation as a gunslinger and who has been wounded in a fight with Laredo Stevens (Bruce Cabot) and his gang. A former associate in crime, Stevens is responsible for the death of Quirt's father and is now out to kill Quirt before Quirt kills him. While riding across the property of the Worth family, Quirt falls from his horse in exhaustion and wakes up several days later finding himself attended by their daughter Prudence (Gail Russell). She is a gentle and pacific Quaker, and therefore a complete contrast to the hard and distrusting Quirt, but she gazes with fondness on him, and he gradually comes under her spell. He recovers his health and partakes of ranch life and chores but vows that he will kill Laredo, and the religious gentility of the Worths cannot change his mind. He leaves them and with a pair of friends destroys property owned by Laredo. Afterwards he surprises his friends by telling them he no longer wishes to continue this kind of life and that he will return to the Worth ranch.

Also in pursuit of Quirt is Marshall McClintock (Harry Carey), who is set to bring Quirt to justice for a long string of offenses. In seeing him settled at the Worth ranch, however, he is willing to give him the benefit of the doubt as Quirt resolves to lead a peaceful life. But McClintock warns him that there is a

Harry Carey, Wayne's mentor and model.

The young boy (Stephen Grant) looks up to the badman as a hero. His sister sees something else.

hangman's noose waiting for him if he steps out of line. By now Quirt is completely in love with Prudence, and he tells her that if she will marry him he will put aside his gun, forget his vow to kill Laredo, and settle down to a peaceful life among the Quakers. Laredo, however, remains intent to catch up with Quirt and kill him. He and his men ambush Quirt and Prudence as they ride in a buggy, and in escaping the gunmen Quirt drives the buggy into a river. Laredo and his men assume the couple have drowned, which is almost true in the case of the delicate Prudence. She becomes deathly ill, which causes Quirt to strap on his gunbelt and go after Laredo, who is known to be in the nearby town. As Quirt is about to settle the score with Laredo, the Worths arrive in an open wagon, with Prudence lying in the back. She has begged them to bring her. Seeing her and again realizing his love for her and the pledge he has made, Quirt turns over his gun to her. As he does so, Laredo takes aim. A shot is heard – but it is a shot made by McClintock as he kills Laredo. The marshall bids good-bye to the family as they drive away with Quirt but he warns him that he is always there to hang him if he ever returns to his former ways. But the badman is now in the hands of the angel.

Although modestly scaled, *Angel and the Badman* is a superior western and an unusual one. It proved a fine start to Wayne's new venture as a producer, and it also revealed his ability to portray a character of more complexity than those in his previous films. That ability would soon be utilized by John Ford and Howard Hawks in a procession of truly remarkable westerns, such as *Red River* (1948), *She Wore a Yellow Ribbon* (1949), and *The Searchers* (1955). Thanks to Wayne's image and character, they are masterpieces of world cinema.

A break in the shooting with writer-director James Edward Grant, Russell, Jack Halloran, and Irene Rich.

149

Harold Lloyd as Harold Diddlebock, the freshman hero of Mad Wednesday.

EIGHT

FUNNY BONES

American humor, like other forms of American expression, is an amalgam of many influences. As an international mecca, Hollywood attracted its talent from every corner of the creative market, although in the area of humor the two strongest strains were British and German. Charlie Chaplin, Stan Laurel, and others brought the traditions of the English music hall, with its emphasis on poignant character humor, while the German slapstick tradition, long a part of American vaudeville, soon found new expression in silent movie comedies. With it all emerged a definite American tendency for verbal quips and sardonic comment, which would have to wait until sound to make its real mark. The sardonic quality would eventually be refined into satire, of which *Life With Father* is a beautiful example, and the quip would find its master in Bob Hope. The blend of slapstick, the quip-attitude, and the poignant character study early found a marvelous outlet in the likable person of Harold Lloyd, a truly representative personality in American comedy.

In 1952 the Academy of Motion Picture Arts and Sciences awarded a special Oscar. Its inscription read: "To Harold Lloyd, master comedian and good citizen." Those few words sum up one of the most remarkable men in the history of films. Along

The freshman years later, no longer a hero, just a disillusioned clerk...

152

with Charlie Chaplin and Buster Keaton, Lloyd was a foundation for the school of American screen comedy. They were the triumvirate clowns of the silent era, and it is doubtful if their skill or appeal will ever be equaled. Each was different and distinct, and whereas Chaplin and Keaton comically pointed up the plight of the "little man" at odds with society and very often a loner, Lloyd made his mark with the image of the nice, average young man, essentially guileless and trusting – and forever getting himself into absurd situations. Some of those situations were hair-raising; Lloyd was his own stuntman and often performed on the edge of high cliffs and the sides of tall buildings, adding heart-in-mouth suspense to his humor. Clean-cut but awkward, with a sunny but rather shy disposition, Lloyd's young man was as likable as he was amusing. Unlike Chaplin and Keaton, who mostly portrayed victims of capricious fate, Lloyd's screen persona was that of a man who triumphed over adversity through idealism and determination. It was an immensely successful image and much of that success was doubtlessly due to the image being an extension of the man. Harold Lloyd was indeed a likable man.

Born in a small town in Nebraska in 1893, Lloyd was smitten with show business as a child and started to make a living as an actor while still in his teens. In 1913 he joined a stock company; after it played Los Angeles, he decided to stay in the city and find work in the movies. All he could get was work as an extra, although he was ingenious enough to turn up in a variety of disguises, and with his make-up case never more than a reach away. He struck up a friendship with a fellow extra named Hal Roach, who one day announced that he had come into a large sum of money and intended opening a studio of his own. He was as good as his word, and hired Lloyd at the then standard rate of three dollars a day but soon upped it to five when Lloyd began to play characters. After doing a multitude of comic bit parts Lloyd signed with Roach to do a series and devised a character named Lonesome Luke, a knockabout tramp-like figure quite unlike the Lloyd image of a few years later. Starting in 1917 Lloyd made more than sixty shorts as Luke but never felt really comfortable in the part. However, his popularity gradually enabled him to dictate his own image, which he decided would be that of an ordinary fellow, but characterized by the wearing of horn-rimmed glasses and a straw hat.

Lloyd's first feature was *A Sailor-Made Man* in 1921. Its success convinced him that the public would accept him as a comic in more than short films, and with his next picture, *Grandma's Boy*, his place in the affections of the moviegoing public was assured. Pictures like *Safety Last* (1923) and *The Freshman* (1925) made him a major public figure and a very wealthy man. Lloyd was one of the few Hollywood personalities of his time who was also a shrewd businessman and knew how to be his own producer. Formed in 1924, Harold Lloyd Productions made its owner a millionaire, and with judicious investments he became one of the landed gentry of Beverly Hills. His sixteen-acre estate and thirty-two-room mansion remain as a splendid reminder of the Golden Age of Hollywood.

Lloyd continued to make films in the sound era but averaged only one every two years, and by 1938, when he made *Professor Beware*, he decided that his film career was over. His interests in other businesses, including charities and a high office with the Shriners, kept him very busy. But in 1945 one of his admirers persuaded him to make another film. Preston Sturges had by this time enjoyed considerable success as a writer-director-producer of a string of brilliantly satiric comedies, and he wanted to do one with Lloyd. Sturges had created new dimensions in comedy with pictures like *The Great McGinty*, *The Lady Eve*, *Sullivan's Travels*, *The Palm Beach Story*, and *Hail the Conquering Hero*, and their success had made him a wealthy man. Always a free-wheeler by nature, and quite a bit eccentric, Sturges decided to cut himself clear from the studio systems he despised and start his own company. In this regard he was greatly encouraged by his friendship with billionaire Howard Hughes, also something of an eccentric, and together they founded California Picture Corporation, with facilities and offices at the Samuel Goldwyn Studios. Since Hughes was also a Lloyd fan he

...and soon an ex-clerk as he gets fired by his boss, E.J. Waggleberry (Raymond Walburn).

supported Sturges's desire to do a Lloyd picture.

Harold Lloyd was presented with a script he couldn't resist. Sturges had not simply written a story that was tailor-made, it was a virtual homage to the great comedian, even to the extent of using the closing scene of Lloyd's classic *The Freshman* as the opening scene of this one, which he called *The Sin of Harold Diddlebock*. *The Freshman* is the story of a genial, innocent, bumbling college boy who yearns to be popular and who finally makes the grade by winning an important football game. Sturges took those exciting and hilarious final moments and spliced in shots of a business tycoon named E.J. Waggleberry (Raymond Walburn) cheering from the stands. He afterwards offers Harold a job with his company, explaining that it is a job at the bottom of the ladder in order to give him the wonderful opportunity to climb that ladder. Says Waggleberry, in a line typical of Sturges's acid humor, "How I envy you – my father unfortunately left me the business." But the joyful start leads to nowhere. Twenty years flash by and Harold is still at the bottom of the ladder. Now he is a shabby, dispirited clerk, and Waggleberry terminates his services, saying, "You not only make the same mistakes year after year, you don't even change your apologies." Harold is given a gold watch in recognition of his twenty years, and he departs, although not until he has said good-bye to office girl Miss Otis (Frances Ramsden), who is but the most recent in the long line of office girls with whom Harold has been in love over the past twenty years.

Soon after leaving Waggleberry's employ, Harold meets an elfin-like hustler named Wormy (Jimmy Conlin), who injects some excitement into Harold's drab life, mostly by getting him drunk and persuading him to part with his life's savings. The former teetotaler goes delightfully berserk under the influence of alcohol. He invests in a glaring plaid suit and proceeds to the racetrack, where he slaps down a one thousand dollar bet on a longshot, which comes in at fifteen–to–one. When he wakes up on Thursday morning he realizes he has no recollection of Wednesday, a day of gaiety and madness in which he apparently bought a circus. Now comes the problem of what to do with it. He decides to descend on the place where money is best represented – Wall Street, and in order to get attention he takes with him a lion on a leash. Harold tells one banker after another that the purchase of a circus will give a change of image, especially if the banker admits children free. During one such visit the lion gets loose and causes Harold, Wormy, and the banker to proceed onto the window ledge of a skyscraper, thereby giving Lloyd and Sturges a chance to revive the breathtaking comic

Harold and friend intimidate banker Jack Norton.

*Harold released from jail with his
girl friend, Frances Ramsden, and
crony, Jimmy Conlin.*

stunts that played such a vital part in the classic Lloyd comedies, particularly *Safety Last.*

After dangling on the side of the high building, and causing Wormy, the banker, and the lion to also dangle, Harold is arrested and put in jail. Miss Otis comes to bail him out and to inform him, to his delight, that one of the things he did during his lost Wednesday was to marry her. Next come all the bankers, now aware of the publicity and bidding with each other to own Harold's circus. But the Ringling Brothers, keen to eliminate competition, make the best offer and hand Harold a check for $175,000. Then Waggleberry enters to offer Harold a partnership in the firm, and all is well. The freshman has finally made it to the top of the ladder, proving that the aphorism he framed and hung over his desk is not in vain: "Everybody's a flop until he's a success."

The Sin of Harold Diddlebock was completed by the spring of 1946 but not released until the following February. And Harold Lloyd was far from pleased with it. The euphoria that triggered the project and the good feelings and mutual admiration between the comedian and the writer-director gradually turned cool, as they later did with Hughes when he saw the results. The three rich men had not become rich by being timid or retiring. They were all strong, assertive men who were used to doing things their own way. Lloyd and Sturges could not agree on

comedic technique and style; in the first few days of shooting Lloyd was able to call the shots but then Sturges began requesting that scenes be filmed both his way and Lloyd's; eventually Lloyd backed down in order to maintain equilibrium and allowed Sturges to do the picture his way. Sturges was pleased with the results, but Hughes was not, especially when the critics gave it only mild reviews and the public showed only mild interest. After a few months Hughes withdrew the film and put it on the shelf. A few months later he and Sturges came to total disagreement while making another film, and it was decided to put an end to California Pictures Corporation.

Howard Hughes, after letting the film sit for a couple of years, pulled out *The Sin of Harold Diddlebock* and decided to reshape it. He trimmed about a dozen minutes out, including one whole sequence featuring Rudy Vallee as a banker, put back a few bits from previous outtakes, and gave it the more arresting title of *Mad Wednesday*. Purists who dote on the magnificent Sturges may claim that his film was butchered, but those who have seen both versions favor the tighter, faster-moving Hughes edition. On the other hand, those who appreciate the work of Harold Lloyd are left wondering what the film would have been like had it been left in his own hands. But if nothing else, *Mad Wednesday* stands as the last – and very amusing – film of a giant of American comedy.

On the set with film executive J.A. Krug, Ramsden, writer-director-producer Preston Sturges, and Lloyd.

Harold Lloyd, the perennial image.

Despite having been born an Englishman, in a London suburb in 1904, Bob Hope is a quintessentially American comic. His stance, his patter, and his personality belong to no other country. He has long gone beyond mere fame. For lack of a better description Hope is a national institution, and his track record as an entertainer of armed forces personnel is legendary. His stamina is incredible. There are few humans who have traveled as much and as constantly or who have enjoyed their work with such a passion. Hope is a workaholic, and for those who have grown up during his half-century of activity he is as familiar, if not more so, than relatives and friends.

No medium of entertainment has eluded Bob Hope. His experience includes nightclubs, vaudeville, the legitimate stage, radio, the movies, television, and stand-up situations in countless nooks and crannies of the world. And he has been a success in all of them. He is a glittering example of the American Dream come true. Born poor, he is now one of the wealthiest men in

Dorothy Lamour and Bob Hope in My Favorite Brunette.

A break in the shooting: assistant director Mel Epstein, director Elliot Nugent, Lamour, and Hope.

Hollywood, and he could not possibly be more famous.

Hope's origins were humble. His stone-mason father took the family to Cleveland, Ohio, when Bob was four. His actual name is Lester Townes Hope, and he did not decide on Bob until 1928, long after he was earning a living as a comic, because it sounded "more like a hi-ya fella name." He left school when he was sixteen and his first job was selling shoes in a Cleveland department store. In the evenings he pursued his interests in becoming an entertainer by taking whatever singing jobs were available. His Welsh mother had seen to it that he learned about singing in the choir of the Presbyterian church she attended. Additionally Bob took dancing lessons from a vaudevillian and picked up small fees on weekends doing spots in neighborhood theatres. Eventually he was able to get bookings on the vaudeville circuits and learned how to be a song-and-dance man in the many dingy theatres around the Midwest. It was in one of these spots in 1927 that Hope was asked by a manager to make an announcement about the coming attractions and in doing so

made some ad-lib comments that amused the audience. He did it the next night and the next, and gradually added material. In so doing he found his niche as an entertainer. It was the birth of Bob Hope as a stand-up verbal comedian.

Hope played the vaudeville road for several years before being seen in New York in *The Ballyhoo of 1932*. He made a good mark for himself and soon afterwards was signed by radio impresario Major Bowes to appear on the air, the success of which started Hope on his long and rewarding association with the airwaves. The following year he was one of the stars of the Jerome Kern musical *Roberta*. In *The Ziegfeld Follies of 1936* he sang the classic Vernon Duke-Ira Gershwin ballad "I Can't Get Started," and Paramount director Mitchell Leisen was so impressed that he hired Hope to appear in his *The Big Broadcast of 1938*. It was in that picture that Hope and Shirley Ross sang the Oscar-winning "Thanks for the Memory," which inevitably became Hope's theme song.

With the success of *The Big Broadcast of 1938*, Hope became a fixture at Paramount Studios. He would stay with them for twenty years and make all of his best films for them. In 1940 his career took a leap forward when Paramount co-starred him with Bing Crosby and Dorothy Lamour in *The Road to Singapore*, a film that was made with no great expectations. The script was first offered to Burns and Allen, who didn't want it, and then to Fred MacMurray and Jack Oakie, who also declined. Hope and Crosby took it just for fun and on the understanding they could ad-lib and improvise. The results were hilarious and launched what would become one of the best loved series of pictures ever made. Much of the value of the playing came from the fact that Hope, Crosby, and Lamour were true friends. The two men had met while they were both appearing at the Capitol Theatre in New York in 1932. It was in the same year that Hope met Dorothy Lamour, when he was a singer at the Hotel One Fifth Avenue. So by the time they came to do *Singapore* eight years

later they were well familiar and more than happy to make a picture together. Over the years there would be roads to Zanzibar, Morocco, Utopia, Rio, Bali, and Hong Kong, and both Hope and Crosby would make other films with Lamour as their co-star. She played opposite Hope in *Caught in the Draft* (1941), *They Got Me Covered* (1943), and, best of all, *My Favorite Brunette* (1947).

In *My Favorite Brunette* Hope is Ronnie Jackson, a baby photographer who wants to become a private detective and has received in the mail his course in detection and his pistol. He also has rigged up a camera which can shoot through keyholes. A real private eye (Alan Ladd in an unbilled guest part) tells Ronnie to watch his office while he goes to Chicago, and not long after he leaves a beautiful girl (Dorothy Lamour) comes in to hire the services of a detective. She is Carlotta Montay and she wants Ronnie to find her rich uncle (Frank Puglia) who disappeared right after arriving from South America. She gives him a map

which he hides, but before he can leave his office, a strange little man called Kismet (Peter Lorre) comes in looking for the map and knocks Ronnie unconscious. When he comes to he follows a planted lead to the gang's headquarters in a California sanitarium and is immediately captured.

Ronnie gives them false instructions on how to find the map, which would lead them to a valuable uranium deposit, and manages to make his escape from the sanitarium in the company of Carlotta. Following a clue smuggled by her uncle they go to New York and get jobs in a hotel where the conspirators have taken rooms and where they try to talk a government official (Reginald Denny) into an unnecessary purchase of the uranium deposits. The poor official winds up dead, and the crooks switch the evidence that Ronnie has collected and make him out to be the killer. Ronnie is arrested, tried, and sentenced to death in the gas chamber of San Quentin.

Ronnie is granted his last request, which is to tell his story to

Scenes from My Favorite Brunette. *From previous pages: Hope and Peter Lorre; Hope, Lamour, and Charles Dingle; Jack La Rue, Jim Pierce, Hope, Lamour, and James Flavin; La Rue, Budd Fine, Hope, Lamour, Flavin, and Dingle; La Rue, John Hoyt, Dingle, Frank Puglia, Lorre, Hope, and Lon Chaney, Jr.*

the gathered newspapermen, and he does after complaining about the quality of the last meal served him. As he gets to the end of his story, Carlotta arrives with the evidence that saves him. Ronnie's keyhole camera paid off, and the shots he took of the actual killing have all turned out well. He is exonerated, at which point the executioner is heard to say, "Oh, darn!" Ronnie looks up and finds the executioner to be Bing Crosby. Ronnie then looks at the audience and says, "He'll play in any kind of picture."

Ronnie Jackson is typical Bob Hope. He is glib and eager for the good life, lecherous and cowardly but always likable. Like all the early Hope comedies, the script of *My Favorite Brunette* is neatly tailored to Hope's style. It moves quickly and is peppered with quips. When setting out on his mission he says, "It takes courage, brains, and a gun to be a detective. I've got the gun."

When realizing the mess the crooks have fixed for him, he yells, "This is the biggest frame-up since Whistler's mother," and when he has trouble climbing a tree, he complains, "It always looked so easy in the Tarzan pictures." But most typical is his reaction when he and Lamour are caught in a dead end in the sanitarium after being chased by the villains, "We're caught like rats in a trap." Then he looks at her beauty and the old glint comes to his eyes: "But I'm a boy rat and you're a girl rat."

Brunette is vintage Hope. When he became the super-busy giant of later years his films suffered as a consequence, but in the forties his pictures received his full attention, and they were given fine production values by Paramount. His supporting cast in this film, for example, is top drawer: Peter Lorre, almost lampooning himself as a foreign spy; Charles Dingle, ever the chilly manipulator; John Hoyt, with his precise diction and suave but cold manner; Lon Chaney, Jr., the warm-hearted goon; Reginald Denny, pompous but obliging; and Jack La Rue, the relentless hood. But best of all, Dorothy Lamour, kindly, supportive, and lovely. They, and the film, are a reminder of a particularly rich time in American movie comedy.

Father and family:
Johnny Calkins,
Martin Milner, Irene
Dunne, William
Powell, Jimmy Lydon,
and Derek Scott.

164

Father, definitely the head of the household: Powell, Scott, Emma Dunn, Lydon, Dunne, and Milner.

Clarence Day was an affluent New Yorker of commanding disposition and imperious personality who flourished in the late nineteenth century and ran his Madison Avenue home in an unyieldingly authoritarian manner. He was an American father of the old, old school and light years removed from the genial dope portrayed in movies and television of the mid-twentieth century. Mr. Day would, however, have vanished in the mists of time but for his son Clarence Jr., who captured his father's character and antics in a book of sketches he called *Life With Father.*

In 1939 Howard Lindsay and Russell Crouse adapted the material into a play, and in that form it ran on Broadway for a solid eight years. Warner Bros. acquired the film rights and hired the esteemed Donald Ogden Stewart to write the screenplay and to be as faithful as possible to the original material, but allowing for the necessary expansion in terms of movement and intimacy for the cameras. The result satisfied all concerned, and the picture received the most deft performance imaginable from William Powell. In fact, Powell was so good as Clarence Day it is hard to think of another actor playing the role. He was fifty-five at the time of filming, and he had been in the movies since 1922. In other words, he had had twenty-five years of acting before cameras, and he was a master. Powell was himself an American gentleman, suave and cultivated, charming in a cool sort of way, and by adding the facade of a man constantly disgusted by human failings, Powell slid comfortably into the character of Clarence Day.

For the role of Mrs. Day, Warners needed an actress who was not only greatly experienced but as much a lady as Powell was a gentleman. The choice quickly narrowed down to Irene Dunne, whose ability to blend humor, gentility, and feminine allure has few equals. Her movie career began in 1930, and in the following decade she won popularity with romantic dramas like *Back Street* (1932) and *The Magnificent Obsession* (1935), and

Father knows best...

romantic comedies like *Theodora Runs Wild* (1936) and *The Awful Truth* (1937). Through it all she remained patrician but amusing and lovable, and she was therefore perfect to play the wife of Clarence Day.

The title *Life With Father* conveys the message. Mr. Day's most oft heard expression is "Gad!" He is perpetually exasperated. Why is there so little efficiency in the world? Why can't others function as ably as he? When he goes to an employment agency to hire a maid he is asked about the character of his home." Proudly he replies, "*I am the character in my home.*" Then he turns to a line of women, points with his cane and says, "I'll take that one."

Maids pass through the Day home fairly swiftly, but his gentle wife Vinnie and his three sons have learned to take his peremptory manner in stride. He is constantly alarmed at his wife's failure to understand financial matters, and in explaining the facts of life to young Clarence (Jimmy Lydon) he declares, "A woman doesn't think. She gets all stirred up." Then, after a few more meaningless words he dismisses the boy with, "Now you know all about women." His wife is forever engaged in circum-navigating his lack of confidence in her ability to run a home. He is astounded when she claims that having a charge account at a store is good business because it lets the store do all the bookkeeping, but there is, as always, method in her madness. Since Father refuses to buy a new suit for their eldest son, Clarence, Vinnie buys an ugly china dog for fifteen dollars, which Father immediately demands be returned to the store. She agrees and says the fifteen dollars will buy the new suit.

...he thinks.

Mother greeting houseguests Elizabeth Taylor and ZaSu Pitts.

"This way it doesn't cost you a penny."

Father is pleased when cousin Cora (ZaSu Pitts) and her daughter Mary (Elizabeth Taylor) come for a visit but alarmed when he hears they will be staying for a few days. "What do they think this is, a hotel?" More pleased than the others is Clarence, who falls in love with the lovely Mary. One evening as they are all having dinner the question of religion comes up as Mary and Clarence hint about marriage and declare the faiths to which they belong. From this conversation emerges the staggering fact that Father was never baptized. His shocked wife tells him it is something he will have to do. Father rejects this notion as womanly nonsense and claims that he and God have been getting along famously, and that he has no intention of getting baptized, now or ever.

Since their father is adverse to giving them pocket money, Clarence and brother John (Martin Milner) take a part-time job selling "Bartlett's Beneficent Balm – a Boon to Mankind," until Father hears of it and tells them he will not have his name disgraced in such a manner. But the attempt at earning money has an unfortunate sad effect. Vinnie falls sick, and believing that the Bartlett Balm will cure her they pour a spoonful into her tea, which causes her to be even more ill. Father, whose love for his wife is deeper than any of his other passions, even his support of the Republican Party, is for the first time in his life reduced to being a common man in his concern for Vinnie. He is willing to promise her anything if God will grant her recovery. Thinking that she is near death Father even agrees to be baptized.

His sons' venture into business results in claims being made against them. The boys have been paid off in product rather than money, and the people whose household pets have been made ill by the balm want their money back. To save his honor Father has to shell out $128 to placate the boys' irate customers. But not without near apoplexy and screams of "tarnation!" His anger soon subsides when Vinnie shows signs of getting better, and once she is fully recovered she keeps him to his promise to be baptized. So one Sunday morning he strides from his house with his family and gets into his carriage. A policeman who knows how Father feels about church asks him where he is going. Yells Father, "I'm going to be baptized, dammit!"

Life With Father remains a delightful cameo of a bygone era and an almost poignant reminder of an American way of life far removed from the present. The danger in looking at it lies in

Edmund Gwenn is the minister mother hopes will baptize her very unwilling husband...

. . . and she finally has her way.

being seduced by its charm and humor into regarding it as a testament to a better time and a finer way of life. Perhaps for Clarence Day and his family it was; for many millions, bereft of civil rights and social security, it was not. A movie must be looked at purely for what it is – entertainment – and that is as true for the so-called realism of today's screen as for the fantasy of the Golden Era of Hollywood. *Life With Father* is a fine movie because of its ingredients and because the ingredients luckily gelled into a beautiful package. It has fine performances by William Powell and Irene Dunne, two of the classiest figures in the history of the American screen, a top-notch script, fine sets and costumes, rich Technicolor, a jaunty score by Max Steiner, skillful direction by Michael Curtiz, and all the expertise of a major studio at its peak. Things could hardly have been better. Sadly the conditions of movie making today are vastly different and painfully more difficult. And the American image has suffered because of it. One hopes today's movie makers might realize that what they put on the screen affects not only the self-regard of their fellow citizens but the image of their country in every part of the world.

The Conestogas helped conquer a continent:
Utah Wagon Trail, a Republic picture.

E P I L O G U E

ENDURING STRENGTHS

The credo of Hollywood in its Golden Age was that life should be more like the movies and not the other way around. It was an attitude that produced the hundreds of movies we now regard as classics. The men who made them, men like Michael Curtiz, John Ford, King Vidor, William Wellman, Howard Hawks, Frank Capra, Fritz Lang, Lewis Milestone, Preston Sturges, and Orson Welles, all of whom are represented in this book, were the architects of filmic Americana, and as such they presented America to the world. They dealt with illusion and fiction for the most part. Their purpose was entertainment, with a little information and inspiration splashed here and there for good measure. Their American images were mostly good ones, inclined toward optimism rather than pessimism, and what they achieved was clearly of value. If not, why do we still honor them and look at their best films with respect and continuing enjoyment?

In the past decade nostalgia has assumed the proportions of an industry. This applies particularly to Hollywood and the movies. Is it due to a longing for the past? a desire to return to former times? a genuine belief that things used to be better? The answers to all these questions are likely to be only a partial affirmative. As many a pundit has pointed out, the good old days weren't really all that good, and most of us are more comfortable

171

The Great Train Robbery, the first western: a tradition begins.

now. Our problems may be greater, but so are our assets.

What is it then for which Americans feel nostalgic? Possibly a sense of loss of innocence, but just what form that innocence took is hard to determine. Life for Americans in this century has been easier than life for people in other countries, but it has never been free of strife, struggle, and uncertainty. But Americans, more than other people, have lived under an idealistic charter, and they have always been encouraged to seek the good life. According to Hollywood the good life was more available in America than elsewhere.

In America people found epic space, epic resources, and epic opportunity. These are the basic American images, backed up by all the epic wordage of the Constitution, the Declaration of Independence, and the Bill of Rights. No other country has such wordage. It was in America that for the first time in history human beings were offered guarantees about life. Freedom was the keynote of those guarantees and it has been a constant theme in American movies right from the start. *The Great Train Robbery* (1903) is, after all, a tip of the hat to free enterprise, and it is worthy of note that no other country has glamorized its outlaws as much as America, although it always sees them put in their place by people with a better sense of decency and justice.

Steve McQueen chasing cattle rustlers in Tom Horn
(©1980 by Warner Bros. Inc.).

But the image of the free-wheeler retains its appeal. More recently *Tom Horn* (1980) celebrates the courage and initiative of a nonconformist and loner of the Old West, played by the late Steve McQueen, himself a nonconformist and loner, but nevertheless sees him hung for his transgressions. The apparent philosophical conclusion is that the good old days are gone forever – but isn't it a damned pity! This is probably the way Americans feel about their way of life, and it more than probably accounts for the two most popular male movie stars in America today being Burt Reynolds and Clint Eastwood. They are still playing the loner, the freedom lover, the nonconformist, and the common man of uncommon initiative. Both are at their best when playing the cheeky rogue and especially endearing when bending the law.

No image is more American than that of a wagon train winding its way across a vast and spectacular landscape. It is more than visual, it is symbolic of the American spirit, the quest for freedom, and the chance to chart one's course by the stars. Americans of today may have accepted the social state and its benefits, but there is still not much evidence of it on the screen. According to Hollywood, Americans don't much care for the idea of government. In the movies Americans like to see them-

selves overcoming their problems without calling on Washington. The dirt poor farmer of *The Southerner* will tackle his problems without federal aid. In *Meet John Doe* incipient fascism is checked on the local level by the common folk, as are the excesses of capitalism in *It's a Wonderful Life*. The most political film in this book is *Our Daily Bread*, in which a group of Depression victims band together, pool their talents, and work for the common good. It is communism of the purest kind, but it has nothing to do with government. These are people who do it *their* way, the Right way, even when it means veering to the Left.

Another American notion that clings, despite evidence to the contrary, is social equality. No human society has ever been free of distinctions, but Americans still like to think they are all middle class. One of the characteristics that makes Thornton Wilder's *Our Town* thoroughly American is the equality of the people in Grovers Corners. In a European story the town doctor and the town's newspaper editor would likely be somewhat remote socially. In *Our Town* they are just plain folks, like everybody else. In *It's a Wonderful Life* the financier played by Lionel Barrymore is powerful but not respected. In a European story he would be a feared and superior figure. Not in an American picture. He simply has money, no real authority. Hollywood has long fostered the American disregard for Authority, and it is a quality, or assumed quality, for which people in other countries have a sneaking admiration. The popularity of John Wayne was not limited to America, and neither is that of Burt Reynolds and Clint Eastwood.

The American image is still one that celebrates freedom, space, and opportunity. It turns sour, as it has in contemporary films, when those virtues are denied or perverted. Today's Hollywood is quick to exploit the sourness, the disillusion, and the cynicism, but for all that Americans still like to think of themselves in terms of John Wayne. Wayne took a rapping from the youngsters in the seventies, but as those youngsters have grown older they tend to share the regret that the Duke is gone. The mood of America as it entered the eighties was markedly conservative.

The election of Ronald Reagan to the highest office in the land is an affirmation of the American return to conservatism. Reagan himself was of the generation of the Hollywood macho giants. He came from that age of American innocence in which a man could make it on his way – without government help or hindrance, by God! Reagan is well in line with the good old American image. He came from a working family, he worked his way through college, excelled at football, got a job as a sports announcer in small-time radio, and worked his way up. In 1937 he had the great good fortune to be signed to a movie contract. What did he play in the movies? Sports announcers, footballers, newspaper reporters (always crusading), cavalrymen, and, in his one classic film, *Kings Row*, he was a small town buck who overcame adversity. What could be more American? The story of Ronald Reagan is itself like a Hollywood movie of the Golden Age. The fact that the American public elected him is strong evidence of an almost desperate yearning for the images of the American past. The fact that such a yearning exists gives hope that all is not lost. The Spirit of '76 may be battered, but it is not moribund.

Bill Williams, Ronald Reagan, and Noah Beery, Jr. in The Last Outpost, *1951.*

CASTS AND CREDITS

JUDGE PRIEST

A Fox Picture, 1934
Produced by Sol Wurtzel
Directed by John Ford
Written by Dudley Nichols and Lamar Trotti
Based on stories by Irvin S. Cobb
Photographed by George Schneiderman
Music by Samuel Kaylin
80 minutes

Brenda Fowler and Will Rogers.

CAST:

Judge William Priest	Will Rogers
Reverend Ashby Brand	Henry B. Walthall
Jerome Priest	Tom Brown
Ellie May Gillespie	Anita Louise
Virginia Maydew	Rochelle Hudson
Senator Maydew	Berton Churchill
Bob Gillis	David Landau
Mrs. Priest	Brenda Fowler
Aunt Dilsey	Hattie McDaniel
Jeff Poindexter	Stepin Fetchit
Flem Tally	Frank Melton
Billy Gaynor	Roger Imhof
Sergeant Jimmy Bagby	Charley Grapewin
Juror number twelve	Francis Ford
Doc Lake	Paul McAllister
Gabby Rives	Matt McHugh
Herman Feldsburg	Hy Meyer
Sheriff Birdsong	Louis Mason

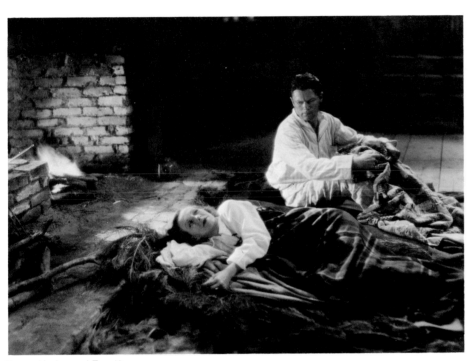

Karen Morley and Tom Keene.

OUR DAILY BREAD

A King Vidor Production, 1934
Released by United Artists
Directed and written by King Vidor
Photographed by Robert Planck
Music by Alfred Newman
80 minutes

CAST:

Mary Sims	Karen Morley
John Sims	Tom Keene
Chris	John Qualen
Sally	Barbara Pepper
Louis	Addison Richards
Barber	Lionel Baccus
Cigar salesman	Harris Gordon
Jew	Bill Engel
Plumber	Frank Minor
Carpenter	Henry Hall
Undertaker	Frank Hammond
Bully	Lynton Brant
Politician	Henry Burroughs
Professor	Harry Bradley
Blacksmith	Captain Anderson
Lawyer	Si Clogg

Thomas Mitchell, William Holden, Martha Scott, Guy Kibbee, and Stuart Erwin.

OUR TOWN

A Principal Artists Picture, 1940
Released by United Artists
Produced by Sol Lesser
Directed by Sam Wood
Written by Thornton Wilder, Frank Craven
and Harry Chandlee
Based on the play by Thorton Wilder
Photographed by Bert Glennon
Music by Aaron Copland
90 minutes

CAST:

Mr. Morgan	Frank Craven
George Gibbs	William Holden
Emily	Martha Scott
Dr. Gibbs	Thomas Mitchell
Mrs. Gibbs	Fay Bainter
Editor Webb	Guy Kibbee
Mrs. Webb	Beulah Bondi
Howie Newsome	Stuart Erwin
Simon Stimson	Philip Wood
Rebecca Gibbs	Ruth Toby
Wally Webb	Douglas Gardiner
Constable	Spencer Charters
Mrs. Soames	Doro Merande
Professor Willett	Arthur Allen
Reverend	Charles Trowbridge
Joe Crowell	Tim Davis
Si Crowell	Dix Davis

Zachary Scott and J. Carrol Naish.

THE SOUTHERNER

A United Artists Release, 1945
Produced by David Loew and Robert Hakim
Directed by Jean Renoir
Written by Jean Renoir
Based on the Novel *Hold Autumn in Your Hand*
by George Sessions Perry
Photographed by Lucien Andriot
Music by Werner Janssen
91 minutes

CAST:

Sam Tucker	Zachary Scott
Nona Tucker	Betty Field
Granny Tucker	Beulah Bondi
Daisy Tucker	Bunny Sunshine
Jot Tucker	Jay Gilpin
Harmie	Percy Kilbride
Ma Tucker	Blanche Yurka
Tim	Charles Kemper
Devers	J. Carroll Naish
Finlay	Norman Lloyd
Doc White	Jack Norworth
Bartender	Nestor Paiva
Lizzie	Estelle Taylor
Party girl	Dorothy Granger
Becky	Noreen Roth
Ruston	Paul Harvey
Uncle Pete	Paul E. Burns

MEET JOHN DOE

A Warner Bros. Picture, 1941
Produced and directed by Frank Capra
Written by Robert Riskin
Photographed by George Barnes
Music by Dimitri Tiomkin
123 minutes

CAST:

John Willoughby	Gary Cooper
Ann Mitchell	Barbara Stanwyck
D.B. Norton	Edward Arnold
Colonel	Walter Brennan
Henry Connell	James Gleason
Mrs. Mitchell	Spring Byington
Mayor Lovett	Gene Lockhart
Ted Sheldon	Rod La Rocque
Beany	Irving Bacon
Bert Hansen	Regis Toomey
Angelface	Warren Hymer
Pop Dwyer	Aldrich Bowker
Mrs. Hansen	Ann Doran
Dan	Sterling Holloway
Mrs. Brewster	Mrs. Gardner Crane
Sourpuss Smithers	J. Farrell MacDonald
Mike	Pat Flaherty

Walter Brennan and Gary Cooper.

Donna Reed and James Stewart.

IT'S A WONDERFUL LIFE

A Liberty Films Production, 1946
Released by RKO Radio Pictures
Produced and directed by Frank Capra
Written by Frances Goodrich, Albert Hackett,
and Frank Capra
Based on the story *The Greatest Gift*
by Philip Van Doren Stern
Photographed by Joseph Walker and Joseph Biroc
Music by Dimitri Tiomkin
129 minutes

CAST:

George Bailey	James Stewart
Mary Hatch	Donna Reed
Mr. Potter	Lionel Barrymore
Uncle Billy	Thomas Mitchell
Clarence	Henry Travers
Mrs. Bailey	Beulah Bondi
Ernie	Frank Faylen
Bert	Ward Bond
Violet Bick	Gloria Grahame
Mr. Gower	H.B. Warner
Sam Wainwright	Frank Albertson
Harry Bailey	Todd Karns
Pa Bailey	Samuel S. Hinds
Cousin Tilly	Mary Treen
Ruth Dakin	Virginia Patton
Cousin Eustace	Charles Williams
Mrs. Hatch	Sara Edwards
Mr. Martini	Bill Edmunds
Annie	Lillian Randolph
Mrs. Martini	Argentina Brunetti

Janet Gaynor and Fredric March.

A STAR IS BORN

A Selznick – International Picture, 1937
Released by United Artists
Produced by David O. Selznick
Directed by William Wellman
Written by Dorothy Parker, Alan Campbell,
and Robert Carson
Based on a story by William Wellman
and Robert Carson
Photographed in Technicolor by W. Howard Greene
Music by Max Steiner
98 minutes

CAST:

Norman Maine	Fredric March
Esther Blodgett/	
Vicki Lester	Janet Gaynor
Oliver Niles	Adolphe Menjou
Lettie	May Robson
Danny McGuire	Andy Devine
Libby	Lionel Stander
Anita Regis	Elizabeth Jenns
Pop Randall	Edgar Kennedy
Casey Burke	Owen Moore
Theodore Smythe	J.C. Nugent
Aunt Mattie	Clara Blandick
Esther's brother	A.W. Sweatt
Miss Philips	Peggy Wood
Harris	Adrian Rosely
Ward	Arthur Hoyt
Posture coach	Guinn "Big Boy" Williams
Otto Friedl	Vince Barnett
Billy Moon	Franklin Pangborn

MY MAN GODFREY

A Universal Picture, 1936
Produced and directed by Gregory La Cava
Written by Morrie Ryskind, Eric Hatch, and
Gregory La Cava
Based on the novel by Eric Hatch
Photographed by Ted Tetzlaff
Music by Charles Previn
93 minutes

CAST:

Godfrey	William Powell
Irene Bullock	Carole Lombard
Angelica Bullock	Alice Brady
Alexander Bullock	Eugene Pallette
Cornelia Bullock	Gail Patrick
Tommy Gray	Alan Mowbray
Molly	Jean Dixon
Carlo	Mischa Auer
George	Robert Light
Mike	Pat Flaherty
Hobo	Robert Perry
Scorekeeper	Franklin Pangborn
Blake	Selmer Jackson

Carole Lombard and William Powell.

NOTHING SACRED

A Selznick – International Picture, 1937
Released by United Artists
Produced by David O. Selznick
Directed by William Wellman
Written by Ben Hecht
Based on a story by James H. Street
Photographed in Technicolor by W. Howard Greene
Musical direction by Lou Forbes
75 minutes

CAST:

Wally Cook	Fredric March
Hazel Flagg	Carole Lombard
Dr. Downer	Charles Winninger
Stone	Walter Connolly
Dr. Figelhoffer	Sig Rumann
M.C.	Frank Fay
Max	Maxie Rosenbloom
Drugstore lady	Margaret Hamilton
Ernest Walker	Troy Brown
Mrs. Walker	Hattie McDaniel
Baggage man	Olin Howard
Photographer	George Chandler
Miss Rafferty	Claire Du Brey
Swede	John Qualen
Mayor	Charles Richman
Dr. Kochinwasser	Alex Schoenberg
Dr. Vunch	Monty Woolley
Dr. Marachuffsky	Alex Novinsky
Mrs. Bullock	Aileen Pringle
Dowager	Hedda Hopper
Moe	Dick Rich

Carole Lombard and Fredric March.

Paulette Goddard and Fred Astaire.

SECOND CHORUS

A Paramount Picture, 1940
Produced by Boris Morros
Directed by H.C. Potter
Written by Elaine Ryan and Ian McClellan
Based on a story by Fred Cavett
Photographed by Theodore Sparkuhl
Musical direction by Ed Paul
84 minutes

CAST:

Danny O'Neill	Fred Astaire
Ellen Miller	Paulette Goddard
Artie Shaw	Himself
J. Lester Chisholm	Charles Butterworth
Hank Taylor	Burgess Meredith
Stu	Frank Melton
Mr. Dunn	Jimmy Conlin
Hotel clerk	Dan Brodie

Barbara Stanwyck, Van Heflin, and Kirk Douglas.

THE STRANGE LOVE OF MARTHA IVERS

A Paramount Picture, 1946
Produced by Hal B. Wallis
Directed by Lewis Milestone
Written by Robert Rossen
Based on a story by Jack Patrick
Photographed by Victor Milner
Music by Miklos Rozsa
117 minutes

CAST:

Martha Ivers	Barbara Stanwyck
Sam Masterson	Van Heflin
Toni Marachek	Lizabeth Scott
Walter O'Neil	Kirk Douglas
Mrs. Ivers	Judith Anderson
Mr. O'Neil	Roman Bohnen
Sam as a boy	Darryl Hickman
Martha as a girl	Janis Wilson
Secretary	Ann Doran
Hotel clerk	Frank Orth
Detective	James Flavin
Walter as a boy	Mickey Kuhn
Special investigator	Charles D. Brown

BLOOD ON THE SUN

A William Cagney Production, 1945
Released by United Artists
Directed by Frank Lloyd
Written by Lester Cole
Based on a story by Garrett Ford
Photographed by Theodore Sparkuhl
Music by Miklos Rozsa
98 minutes

CAST:

Nick Condon	James Cagney
Iris Hilliard	Sylvia Sidney
Ollie Miller	Wallace Ford
Edith Miller	Rosemary De Camp
Colonel Tojo	Robert Armstrong
Prime Minister Tanaka	John Emery
Hijikata	Leonard Strong
Prince Tatsugi	Frank Puglia
Captain Oshima	Jack Halloran
Kajioka	Hugh Ho
Tomamoto	Philip Ahn
Hayoshi	Joseph Kim
Yamada	Marvin Miller
Joseph Cossell	Rhys Williams
Arthur Bicket	Porter Hall
Charley Sprague	James Bell
Amah	Grace Lem
Chinese servant	Oy Chan
Hotel manager	George Paris
Johnny Clark	Hugh Beaumont

Leonard Strong, Jack Halloran, James Cagney, and Marvin Miller.

191

Cary Grant, Gene Lockhart, Alma Kruger, Rosalind Russell,
Regis Toomey, and Cliff Edwards.

HIS GIRL FRIDAY

A Columbia Picture, 1940
Produced and directed by Howard Hawks
Written by Charles Lederer
Based on the play *The Front Page*
by Ben Hecht and Charles MacArthur
Photographed by Joseph Walker
Music direction by Morris Stoloff
92 minutes

CAST:

Walter Burns	Cary Grant
Hildy Johnson	Rosalind Russel
Bruce Baldwin	Ralph Bellamy
Sheriff Hartwell	Gene Lockhart
Mollie Molloy	Helen Mack
Murphy	Porter Hall
Roy Bensinger	Ernest Truex
Endicott	Cliff Edwards
Mayor	Clarence Kolb
McCue	Roscoe Karns
Wilson	Frank Jenks
Sanders	Regis Toomey
Diamond Louie	Abner Biberman
Duffy	Frank Orth
Earl Williams	John Qualen
Mrs. Baldwin	Alma Kruger
Joe Pettibone	Billy Gilbert
Warden Conley	Pat West
Dr. Egelhoffer	Edwin Maxwell
Gus	Irving Bacon

SWING HIGH, SWING LOW

A Paramount Picture, 1937
Produced by Arthur Hornblow, Jr.
Directed by Mitchell Leisen
Written by Virginia Van Upp and
Oscar Hammerstein II
Based on the play *Burlesque*
by George Manker Watters and Arthur Hopkins
Photographed by Ted Tetzlaff
Music direction by Boris Morros
92 minutes

CAST:

Maggie King	Carole Lombard
Skid Johnson	Fred MacMurray
Harry	Charles Butterworth
Ella	Jean Dixon
Anita Alvarez	Dorothy Lamour
Harvey Dexter	Harvey Stephens
Murphy	Cecil Cunningham
Georgie	Charlie Arnt
Henri	Franklin Pangborn
The Don	Anthony Quinn
Purser	Bud Flanagan
Tony	Charles Judels
Police Chief	Harry Semels
Interpreter	Ricardo Mandia
Judge	Enrique DeRosas

Carole Lombard and Fred MacMurray.

LADY OF BURLESQUE

A Hunt Stromberg Production, 1943
Released by United Artists
Directed by William Wellman
Written by James Gunn
Based on the novel *The G-String Murders*
by Gypsy Rose Lee
Photographed by Robert De Grasse
Music by Arthur Lange
Songs by Sammy Cahn and Harry Akst
91 minutes

CAST:

Dixie Daisy	Barbara Stanwyck
Biff Brannigan	Michael O'Shea
S.B. Foss	J. Edward Bromberg
Gee Gee Graham	Iris Adrian
Dolly Haxter	Gloria Dickson
Lolita La Verne	Victoria Faust
Princess Nirvena	Stephanie Bachelor
Inspector Harrigan	Charles Dingle
Alice Angel	Marion Martin
Officer Kelly	Eddie Gordon
Russell Rogers	Frank Fenton
Mandy	Pinky Lee
Stacchi	Frank Conroy
Hermit	Lew Kelly
Sandra	Claire Carlton
Janine	Janis Carter
Louis Grindero	Gerald Mohr
Jake	George Chandler
Sammy	Bert Hanlon

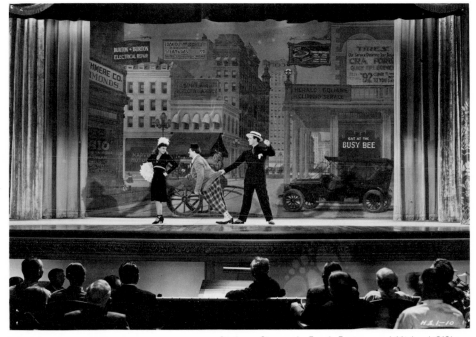

Barbara Stanwyck, Frank Fenton, and Michael O'Shea.

Olivia De Havilland, Errol Flynn, and Ronald Reagan.

SANTA FE TRAIL

A Warner Bros. First National Picture, 1940
Produced by Hal B. Wallis
Directed by Michael Curtiz
Written by Robert Buckner
Photographed by Sol Polito
Music by Max Steiner
110 minutes

CAST:

Jeb Stuart	Errol Flynn
Kit Carson Halliday	Olivia De Havilland
John Brown	Raymond Massey
George Armstrong Custer	Ronald Reagan
Tex Bell	Alan Hale
Bob Halliday	William Lundigan
Rader	Van Heflin
Jason Brown	Gene Reynolds
Cyrus Halliday	Henry O'Neill
Windy Brody	Guinn (Big Boy) Williams
Oliver Brown	Alan Baxter
Martin	John Litel
Robert E. Lee	Moroni Olsen
Phil Sheridan	David Bruce
Barber	Hobart Cavanaugh
Major Sumner	Charles D. Brown
Kitzmiller	Joseph Sawyer
James Longstreet	Frank Wilcox
Townley	Ward Bond
Shoubel Morgan	Russell Simpson
Jefferson Davis	Erville Alderson

Edgar Buchanan and Randolph Scott.

ABILENE TOWN

A Jules Levey Production, 1946
Released by United Artists
Directed by Edwin L. Marin
Written by Harold Shumate
Based on the novel *Trail Town*
by Ernest Haycox
Photographed by Archie J. Stout
Music by Nat W. Finston
90 minutes

CAST:

Dan Mitchell	Randolph Scott
Rita	Ann Dvorak
Bravo Trimble	Edgar Buchanan
Sherry Balder	Rhonda Fleming
Henry Dreiser	Lloyd Bridges
Big Annie	Helen Boyce
Ed Balder	Howard Freeman
Charlie Fair	Richard Hale
Jet Younger	Jack Lambert
Doug Nell	Hank Peterson
Ryker	Dick Curtis
Hazelhurst	Earl Schench
Hannaberry	Eddy Waller

ANGEL AND THE BADMAN

A Republic Picture, 1947
Produced by John Wayne
Directed and written by James Edward Grant
Photographed by A.J. Stout
Music by Richard Hageman
100 minutes

CAST:

Quirt Evans	John Wayne
Prudence	Gail Russell
Wistful McClintock	Harry Carey
Laredo Stevens	Bruce Cabot
Mrs. Worth	Irene Rich
Randy McCall	Lee Dixon
Dr. Mangrum	Tom Powers
Thomas Worth	John Halloran
Johnny Worth	Stephen Grant
Lila Neal	Joan Barton
Frederick Carson	Paul Hurst
Ward Withers	Craig Woods
Nelson	Marshall Reed
Bradley	Olin Howlin

John Wayne and Gail Russell.

197

MAD WEDNESDAY

A California Pictures Corporation Production, 1947
Released by United Artists
Reedited version released by RKO Radio Pictures
Produced, directed, and written by Preston Sturges
Photographed by Robert Pittack
Music by Werner Richard Heymann
Original version: 89 minutes
Reedited version: 78 minutes

CAST:

Harold Diddlebock	Harold Lloyd
Miss Otis	Frances Ramsden
Wormy	Jimmy Conlin
E.J. Waggleberry	Raymond Walburn
Bartender	Edgar Kennedy
Manicurist	Arline Judge
Franklin	Franklin Pangborn
Max	Lionel Stander
Flora	Margaret Hamilton
James R. Smoke	Jack Norton
Jeremiah P. Blackston	Arthur Hoyt
Banker	Julius Tannen
McDuffy	Robert Dudley
Circus manager	Al Bridge
Algernon the coachman	Robert Greig
Bearded lady	Georgia Caine
Barber	Torben Meyer
Seal trainer	Vic Potel
Mike the cop	Frank Moran
Snake charmer	Gladys Forrest

Harold Lloyd, Jimmy Conlin, and Jack Norton.

MY FAVORITE BRUNETTE

A Paramount Picture, 1947
Produced by Daniel Dare
Directed by Elliott Nugent
Written by Edmund Beloin and Jack Rose
Photographed by Lionel Lindon
Music by Robert Emmett Dolan
87 minutes

CAST:

Ronnie Jackson	Bob Hope
Carlotta Montay	Dorothy Lamour
Kismet	Peter Lorre
Willie	Lon Chaney, Jr.
Dr. Lundau	John Hoyt
Major Montague	Charles Dingle
James Collins	Reginald Denny
Baron Montay	Frank Puglia
Miss Rogers	Ann Doran
Prison Warden	Willard Robertson
Tony	Jack La Rue
Crawford	Charles Arnt

Lon Chaney, Jr. and Bob Hope.

William Powell.

LIFE WITH FATHER

A Warner Bros. Picture, 1947
Produced by Robert Buckner
Directed by Michael Curtiz
Written by Donald Ogden Stewart
Based on the play by Howard Lindsay and
Russell Crouse
Photographed in Technicolor
by Peverell Marley and William V. Skall
Music by Max Steiner
118 minutes

CAST:

Father Clarence	William Powell
Vinnie	Irene Dunne
Mary	Elizabeth Taylor
The Reverend Dr. Lloyd	Edmund Gwenn
Cora	ZaSu Pitts
Clarence	Jimmy Lydon
Margaret	Emma Dunn
Dr. Humphries	Moroni Olsen
Mrs. Whitehead	Elizabeth Risdon
Harlan	Derek Scott
Whitney	Johnny Calkins
John	Martin Milner
Anne	Heather Wilde
Policeman	Monte Blue
Nora	Mary Field
Maggie	Queenie Leonard
Delia	Nancy Evans
Miss Wiggins	Clara Blandick
Dr. Somers	Frank Elliott

BIBLIOGRAPHY

Behlmer, Rudy. *Hollywood's Hollywood*. Secaucus, NJ: Citadel Press, 1975.

Chierichetti, David. *Hollywood Director: The Career of Mitchell Leisen*.
New York: Curtis Film Series, 1973.

Cowie, Peter. *The Cinema of Orson Welles*. Cranbury, NJ:
A.S. Barnes and Co., 1974.

Druxman, Michael. *Paul Muni, His Life and His Films*. Cranbury, NJ: A.S. Barnes and Co., 1974.

Gelman, Howard. *The Films of John Garfield*. Secaucus, NJ: Citadel
Press, 1975.

Green, Stanley, and Goldblatt, Burt. *Starring Fred Astaire*. Garden City, NY: Doubleday, 1977.

Jensen, Paul M. *The Cinema of Fritz Lang*. London: Tantivy Press, 1969.

Place, J.A. *The Non-Western Films of John Ford*. Secaucus, NJ: Citadel Press, 1979.

Renoir, Jean. *My Life and My Films*. New York: Atheneum, 1974.

Scherle, Victor, and Levy, William Turner. *The Films of Frank Capra*.
Secaucus, NJ: Citadel Press, 1977.

Sennett, Ted. *Lovers and Lunatics*. New Rochelle, NY: Arlington House, 1973.

Shipman, David. *The Great Movie Stars: The Golden Years*. New York: Bonanza, 1970.

Thomas, Tony. *The Films of Kirk Douglas*. Secaucus, NJ: Citadel Press, 1972.

Ursini, James. *Preston Sturges, An American Dreamer*. New York: Curtis Film Series, 1973.

Vidor, King. *A Tree Is a Tree*. New York: Harcourt Brace, 1953.

Meet John Doe:
Barbara Stanwyck and Gary Cooper.

The making of A Star Is Born: Janet Gaynor first arrives in Hollywood at Grauman's Chinese Theatre.

I N D E X

Titles and page numbers for illustrations are in italic type, names and text references are in roman type. A page number reference in italic parenthesis indicates both text reference and illustration are found on the same page.

My Man Godfrey: *Carole Lombard, William Powell, and Gail Patrick.*

The making of Swing High, Swing Low: *director Mitchell Leisen, Carole Lombard, Jean Dixon, Fred MacMurray, and crew.*

LEARNING RESOURCES

CENTER

ILLINOIS CENTRAL COLLEGE

MCMLXVI

East Peoria, Illinois